WRECKING BALL

BILLY VUNIPOLA
WRECKING BALL

A BIG LAD FROM A SMALL ISLAND:

MY STORY SO FAR

With Gershon Portnoi

HEADLINE

First published in 2017
by HEADLINE PUBLISHING GROUP

Cataloguing in Publication Data is available from the British Library

Hardback ISBN 978 1 4722 4391 1

Typeset in Bliss Light by Jouve (UK), Milton Keynes

Printed and bound in Great Britain by CPI Group (UK) Ltd, Croydon, CR0 4YY

FSC
www.fsc.org

MIX
Paper from
responsible sources
FSC® C104740

Headline's policy is to use papers that are natural, renewable and
recyclable products and made from wood grown in sustainable forests.
The logging and manufacturing processes are expected to conform
to the environmental regulations of the country of origin.

HEADLINE PUBLISHING GROUP
An Hachette UK Company
Carmelite House
50 Victoria Embankment
London EC4Y 0DZ

www.headline.co.uk
www.hachette.co.uk

*For my grandad, Sione, whose dream it was for us
to set up a life for ourselves in the UK; not just to give us
opportunities, but also to help others.*

CONTENTS

1.	Faith, Family and Rugby	1
2.	Broccoli for Breakfast	23
3.	Wrecking Ball Jr	42
4.	Pie and Crash	67
5.	Breaking Bad	92
6.	On the Run	121
7.	Fat and Homeless	144
8.	My Big Tongan Head	168
9.	Losing My Religion	193
10.	Dark Places	214
11.	Being Billy Vunipola	238
	Epilogue	269
	Author's acknowledgements	273
	Picture credits	275
	Index	277

Chapter 1

Faith, Family and Rugby

I'm sitting in the back of the car with Mako. I stuff a large, greasy chip coated in delicious curry sauce into my mouth and chew on it contentedly until it's pulped into nothingness and slides down my throat. Almost before that's happened, my hand is automatically reaching for another chip and I repeat the process.

I'm aware of a commotion in the front of the car. There are raised voices from my mum, in the passenger seat, and my dad, who's driving.

I take another chip. It tastes better than the last one. And the one before that. But not as good as the next one will taste.

Do they taste so good because we won? Or because we won and we both scored a couple of tries each? I'm not sure it makes a difference. Chips and curry sauce will always taste heavenly.

There are some angry words being shouted in our direction in the back of the car. But probably at another driver. Not at us. We won. We played well.

Another chip. And another.

More shouting in the front.

'You two think you're the boys,' says my dad.

Yes we do. And we are. I think that too. Good, we are in agreement. I can carry on eating my chips. But why is he shouting these things at us?

'Everyone else is running around, and you two might as well have been standing on the sideline.'

As I destroy another three chips, I am becoming concerned and am sensing this is not a situation that is going to end in a way which will see me finishing these chips. Little do I know, but it might not be a situation that ends in a way in which I finish the journey.

It goes quiet. Things are calmer. I can finish my chips in peace. Mako has finished his and his head is leaning back on the seat and his eyes are shut.

Sleep is a great idea right now. Sleep is always a great idea anytime. But it feels so right after chips. We're in the car, it's a long journey home, and there's nothing else to do anyway.

I lean my head back on the seat, just like Mako. It doesn't take long for my eyes to close. They're always up for a break too.

What was that? Nothing. It was me falling asleep. I'm drifting. Drifting off to sleep. This is nice. I can sleep 'til we get home. Lovely.

● ● ●

'What are you doing?' says my mum. 'Are you crazy? They're only kids!'

Who's she talking about? What's she talking about? Why am I thinking anything? Hang on, I'm awake. We must be home. I can see my dad and he's waking Mako up and getting him out of the car. So why's mum upset then? She never gets upset when we get home and get out of the car.

I rub my eyes. I do a double take out of the window. We're not home. We've stopped in the middle of the road for no reason I can think of.

Mako's out of the car, and suddenly my door is open and my dad is getting me out of the car and on to the road.

'Why are you doing this?' pleads my mum. 'They were sleeping!'

We're not sleeping anymore as I shiver a bit on the cold street.

I can feel my fear rising as my dad stands in front of us. What now?

'You two jog home in front of the car,' he says, as if that's the most natural thing in the world. As if that's the way we always finish our car journeys.

'Please don't make them do this,' says mum from the car.

'Jog home, I'll drive behind you,' he says.

I'm going to cry. I'm about to bawl my eight-year-old eyes out, because I know that this is so unfair and that other eight-year-olds don't have to do this. The kids in my school wouldn't even believe me if I told them I had to do this. Come to think of it, even I don't believe I have to do this.

I look at Mako and he's sobbing. It helps me to not cry because he is. He knows that it doesn't matter that I am eight and he is ten. We have to run. And we have to run now.

I set off behind Mako, in case he lashes out at me for going ahead of him because I'm a bit fitter and more mobile than him. I'm not saying I'm fit and mobile, just a bit more so than him.

I'm hating this whole thing, but I just want to get it done.

Mako is still crying. In the car behind us, my mum is crying as my dad

3

drives painfully slowly while we run up the hill towards our house which must be around a mile away. But I'm eight and a mile doesn't really mean anything to me – it's a grown-up word and it could take us either two minutes or two hours to jog a mile. Who knows?

'Is my dad actually for real?' I think to myself as I listen to Mako's sobs in front of me, but I say nothing and just focus on getting home.

Hoots and beeps and all sorts come from the cars behind ours, but my dad doesn't care and crawls behind us as we run slowly towards home.

'This guy really is crazy,' I think. And I keep thinking it as we trot on and on and on. We are not adults. We may be the size of adults, but we are children, and this run kills more and more with every step.

We have just played a game of rugby. And eaten a portion of chips. And fallen asleep. Nobody in their right mind would go for a jog after that trilogy.

The ordeal lasts for what seems like hours, although it's probably over in little more than ten minutes. But it's horrible. It's awful. It's upsetting. It hurts.

But the truth is, without all those feelings, I won't get to become an international rugby player.

● ● ●

At the time, that was probably the worst day of my life. When you're a kid, you don't have any perspective. Now, I can laugh about it but I understand that's the way I deal with tough episodes from my childhood. The fact is, we had won the game that day playing for our team New Panteg

Under-11s and we had both gone over twice. But we had also spent huge chunks of the afternoon aimlessly wandering around in our own half watching the action on the other side of the pitch. To us, that was rugby. When the ball came near us, we would perform. Whether that was steamrollering through opponents, or spinning a twenty-metre pass out to the back line – we were interested when play came to us.

The funny thing is I wasn't even supposed to be playing in this team. It was an Under-11 side and I was at least two years too young for it, but thanks to my size I could play alongside Mako and our mate Taulupe Faletau, or Toby as everyone in our adopted home town Pontypool knew him.

Toby played rugby differently to us back then. In fact, he played it pretty much the same way he plays it now. He followed play, chased after the ball, the game, the opposition, whatever it was – he chased it. He didn't stand around looking gormless in his own half, embarrassing his father.

And that was the point. My dad would have considered our performances humiliating to everything he stood for as a pro rugby player, a parent and proud Tongan. To my dad, it wasn't about scoring tries, winning matches and looking good. It was about how hard we worked, how much we wanted it and he felt we made him look stupid because his boys were just strolling around without a care in the world while everyone else was doing the hard work.

He was steaming way before the match had finished, let alone when we were in the car eating our chips. I wouldn't be surprised if my mum had had to stop him from making us run all the way home from the game. Although given that it was a forty-five-minute drive, that might have been a tad extreme, even for my dad. I think they both knew what he had up his sleeve, hence the front seat vocals on the way home.

When you're an eight-year-old, you only look at a small part of the picture, never the whole. That's why I can now say that what my dad did made me into an England rugby player. As hard as it would be for the eight-year-old me to see it, he was right. I may have learned the hard way, but I learned. When you run up a hill in front of your mum and dad's car after a game of rugby with your brother bawling alongside you, you're unlikely to stand around watching a game go by again.

Having said that, sometimes it took me longer to learn every lesson in life. When it came to discipline during my childhood, it's fair to say that I was something of a repeat offender. In fact, they could have locked me up and thrown away the key. Sometimes, or always, I just could not help myself. It was usually impulsive, silly behaviour rather than anything malevolent, but there would rarely be a day that went by without me getting involved in some kind of scrape, whether at school or home. Or both.

Unlike my erratic behaviour, my upbringing was a fairly simple Tongan one. Albeit a simple Tongan upbringing that was spent in Wales and then south west England. My life was all about three things: faith, family and rugby. In that order. Religion is at the heart of every Tongan family's life. Even more so with mine, as my mum eventually became a minister of her own church. In fact, she was the first Tongan to ever be ordained in the UK.

As a kid, Sundays were all about church and eating. You can't have one without the other. We'd all be kicked out of bed at 9am so we had time to get ready for church which started at 10.30am. And without fail, every single week we'd still manage to be late. But that's the Tongan style. Nothing starts at the time it's supposed to. Time is just not that important when you're on a small island in the middle of the Pacific Ocean. We're just more laid back about that kind of thing.

Church would be followed by an enormous family feast. Back home in Tonga, that means pigs would be roasted in the underground ovens for six hours so that they would be ready by the time we returned from church. And then the feast would begin. In Pontypool, it was the same idea but it was just ever so slightly cold outside so there was less underground oven, and more 'get the hell indoors as soon as possible' because we were all so freezing.

But, somehow, despite the weather, we were able to carry on our traditional Tongan lifestyle here while also adapting to the customs of our newly adopted country. When my dad first set foot in Pontypool back in 1998, it was his first taste of life in the United Kingdom. He had grown up on a diet of amazing stories about the Great British Empire, how Captain Cook had turned up in Tonga in the eighteenth century, and the very strong impression Britain had made on him, and all his peers, in their youth.

In school, he was taught how Britain was viewed on a par with the Roman Empire. One of the greatest civilisations the world had known. The winners of the two world wars. Cook and Winston Churchill, the greatest of men. To my dad when he was an islander child, he might have considered it possible that he would one day visit New Zealand or Australia which were relatively close by. But he would never in his wildest dreams have conceived of seeing Britain at any point in his life. To him,

Britain stood for everything that was just and right in the world. He imagined a vast, lush land of immense size and quality with polite, respectful and decent people.

Yet, as he looked around Pontypool twenty-five years later, with all due respect to our first port of call in wonderful Wales, he was bitterly disappointed. It was October, and the weather was foul. Grey skies offered no hint of redemption. A constant drizzle was in the air. But, worst of all, it was indescribably cold for a man who had no experience of a northern hemisphere late autumnal day.

He was alone at first, but eventually, me, Mako, my older sister Tiffany, my younger sister Ana and my mum all joined him so that we could be miserable and cold together. Which is a joke, of course. Growing up in Wales were some of the happiest times of my life. Faith, family and rugby were all we needed and we had plenty of all three.

● ● ●

I'm sitting at the dinner table chomping on some chicken. We're all there. Mum, Dad, Tiffany, Mako, Ana and me. Tonight, it's fried chicken and chips. It's so good. It's always so good. How can it not be good? There's lots of contented munching and crunching around the table. Mum and Dad look happy, but they're eating. They always look happy when they're eating. This is how it is every night. Our family sitting down together as one, to eat and talk.

The talking usually starts with the Devotion and tonight is no exception. It's Mako's turn, which means he chooses a verse from the bible and tells us what it means and why it's significant for him. We're kids, but we take this stuff seriously.

Mum's talking now.

'It's so nice to see you guys again. Thank God everyone is looking so healthy and we pray you stay that way.'

'Amen!' we chorus in response to my mum's prayer.

'Billy!' says my dad.

He says it in a way that suggests he may not be about to lavish praise upon me. To tell me what an exemplary child I am and how my teachers have been waxing lyrical about me. No, he says it in a way which means only one thing. Trouble.

'What have I done now?' I think.

A lot of things I have done immediately spring to mind, but I'm not about to volunteer any of them at this point. Let's just see where this is going.

'Yes, Dad,' I reply.

His stare is fixed on me. There is no escape.

'We got a letter from your school . . .'

OK, perhaps I've misjudged this one. Maybe it's not so bad after all. Someone might have seen fit to let my parents know that I'm actually quite bright, that I get on with everyone, and that I'm generally a decent student. 'Dear Mr & Mrs Vunipola, Just wanted to let you know that Billy is doing fine at school. Love, his teachers.' Yeah, that's exactly the sort of letter that the school usually takes the trouble to write to parents. What on earth am I thinking?

'It says you've been messing around again,' continues my dad as I look down, aware that everyone is looking at me. As if the school would write to

my parents to tell them something good. I know how this ends, and it doesn't end well. The reason I know how this ends is because this happens fairly often. A casual observer would say this happens most evenings. It's almost funny. Almost.

'. . . you've been talking back to the teachers and playing the fool again,' he goes on, reading my charge sheet. But there won't be a trial. I won't be entitled to representation or a fair hearing. This case is closed. And I'm sentenced to the same punishment every time. A good hiding.

My mum takes out the wooden spoon and invites me into the other room. I follow her in, obediently hold out my hands, palms up, and wait for her to rap me hard.

As I wait, I realise it's this bit that's the worst. Don't get me wrong, I don't relish the pain and the sting on my hand when that spoon strikes. Far from it. But these moments, these split seconds, of the anticipation of the pain are somehow worse than actually being hit.

And now, as I stand waiting for the spoon, I'm thinking the same thing I always think. 'Why do I continue to do these stupid things?'

Yes, I'm guilty. That's why there's no need for a trial or any representations on my part. I'm guilty because I always do these daft things, and then immediately regret them. So why do I do them in the first place? I don't frigging know! If I knew that, I wouldn't do them and I wouldn't be standing here waiting for a wooden spoon to strike the palms of my han . . . Smash! The spoon comes down firmly on the tight skin of my right hand and I wince. The pain is sharp and stings like hell. It brings a tear to my eye.

I look at my mum. She has a face full of remorse, pity and sorrow but she sticks to her task as a parent solemnly and resolutely. My face is a sea of

salty tears and as soon as we're done, I trudge off to my bedroom, discon-
solate and distraught.

• • •

At around about that time, once I was safely on my bed with my head in my pillow, I would rage to nobody in particular about how much I hated my parents and threaten to call the NSPCC on them. I never did. I accepted the punishments for what they were. I may not be a parent, but I can now reflect that it takes a very different kind of love to discipline a child the way my parents disciplined me. My parents obviously loved me, but if they'd loved me too much and just let me do whatever the hell I wanted, that would not be love. That would be neglect.

I talk about it with my parents now and we laugh about it. For them, it was their upbringing. They grew up in very traditional Tongan families and were used to getting disciplined and told in no uncertain terms which things were right and wrong. I completely understand that kids are not being brought up like that anymore – kids at my school would say to me, 'Yeah, I got smacked on the bottom last night' and I'd come back to them with 'Mate, I wish I got smacked on the bottom.'

But despite the differences, I'm convinced the way I was brought up worked for me. I was hard to handle as a child. I was rebellious, cheeky and mischievous. I couldn't help myself. The truth is I was often just plain stupid and didn't think things through. My brother was way more calcu-lating than me. Even nowadays, I sometimes say stupid stuff. But usually, I say it for a reaction. As a kid if you say something for a reaction, you'll normally get a big one, but as an adult nobody really cares what I say. Or at least they're too mature to over-react to it. I truly think that if I had never been disciplined in such a strong way by my parents, I have no idea exactly where I'd be right now, but you might find me living in a dumpster somewhere. I would almost certainly not be an international rugby player.

Ask him now, and my dad says he always knew Mako and I were capable of playing rugby at the highest level. It was in our genes, and as a professional himself, he knew how to guide us in the right direction. But in truth that was the last thing he wanted for us. What he really wanted when we were young, was for us to benefit from an amazing education and gain professional qualifications so we could become doctors, lawyers or teachers. That was my dad's dream. And that's why he did everything he could to dissuade us from pursuing a career in rugby – including making us run hill sprints in sub-freezing snow one evening.

● ● ●

The Rock slams his head into Triple H's chest, and my brother and I gasp with delight. We love this! Before we know it, Triple H has The Rock in a headlock, but The Rock escapes and punches H straight on the jaw.

'Woah!' says Mako.

'Sweet!' I say.

I don't understand how these guys don't get hurt more. There's never any blood. They must be superhuman.

Suddenly, we're on the floor in front of the telly that's still showing The Rock and Triple H grappling, but we're now wrestling ourselves and it's awesome as we roll all over the floor, trying to smash each other. This is the only thing that's actually better than watching wrestling. Although it does seem to hurt us a bit more than the guys on TV.

But it's such fun. And it doesn't really matter that we're supposed to be doing our homework right now.

The rules every day are the same. We chill out for a couple of hours after school and then do our homework at 6.30pm. It's now 7pm but what does that matter when we're wrestling?

I'm on the floor and Mako has climbed onto the sofa, in an attempt to replicate The People's Elbow, one of The Rock's signature moves. He launches himself off the couch with his arm at right angles, elbow protruding and makes the perfect landing – right on my throat.

'Arrrrgghhhhh!' I scream, at the precise moment that my dad says 'Kids! Get changed!'

Where the hell did he come from? And why do the people who The Rock elbows never get as hurt as I just did from Mako's elbow? Woah! Maybe Mako is stronger than The Rock? Awesome! Although my throat really hurts right now.

Hang on a sec. What did my dad just say? Did he say get changed? What's he talking about? I look up from the floor, still reeling a bit from The People's Elbow.

My dad is staring at us. He doesn't look angry, but he does look like he means business. My brain's trying to take in so many things at the moment.

'Get changed for what?' I say.

'We're going running,' says Dad.

There must be some mistake here. This can't be right. It's winter outside. *Snow and ice, everything. We can barely get to school in the morning, never mind running. And I hate running anyway. I hate it in any weather.*

'Dad, it's so cold!' *I protest, as Mako heads off to get changed. Why does he just accept these things? Why doesn't he say stuff like me?*

'Shouldn't you be doing your homework now? That's why we're going training. And you're not allowed to watch wrestling.'

He's right about the wrestling. A story did the rounds about a kid who got paralysed while trying to copy one of his favourite wrestler's signature moves and that was enough for it to be banned in our house.

While I ponder that, my mum starts screaming at my dad. Is this a reprieve for us? 'No! You can't take them running now,' *she says.* 'It's freezing, they'll catch colds.' *I could've written her script. It's beautiful and perfect and it's going to get us out of a terrible ordeal. What's got into his head to even make him think this is a good idea?*

Come on, Mum. We can do this.

'It's homework time and they were watching wrestling and fighting,' *he says.* 'They have to learn.'

What are we going to learn by running in the snow? That Wales is absolutely freezing in the winter? I already know that. I'm actually going to learn much more than that, but I don't know that. My mum doesn't know that. But it doesn't matter.

It doesn't matter because Dad has decided this is what's happening so it's happening. Nobody's going to change his mind.

Oh crap.

I get changed. We go outside. It's pitch black, freezing beyond belief, and sleet, hail and Lord knows what else are falling as we make our way to the foot of the hill behind our house.

The breath coming out of our mouths is visible. This was the same trick of nature that used to thrill me when we first arrived in the UK. I loved that, there was nothing cooler than being able to see your own breath. But there's nothing cool about it now. I don't want to see my own breath now, I want to go indoors. I'll do my homework if I have to, I just want to go indoors.

But this is going to happen. It is actually happening. I begin to cry. I'm just a kid, I don't want to do this. Mako is crying too, and my dad hugs us underneath his enormously broad shoulders. Our faces are protected from the elements by his armpits. But this is the only concession he will make.

'Dad, it's so cold!' pleads Mako, as the biting wind tears right through the three of us.

'I know,' he says.

He can't back down now. He can't show us any weakness. Especially as he's now feeling so vulnerable himself. I don't know this but on the inside, my dad is worried. He is so worried about how we are going to survive as a family. His contract with Pontypridd is almost up. It's a Thursday night and he's just found out that he's not playing on Saturday. Not just that, he's not even on the bench. He won't receive a match fee or a potential win bonus. He is confused and concerned. And he wants to teach us a lesson that being a rugby pro is tough, brutal and uncompromising. Like running up the steepest of hills in the worst of weather. Is this what we really need? At this moment, absolutely not.

'You do it ten times, I'll do twenty,' he says as we look up at the hill through wet eyes of sleet, snow and tears.

Oh crap. Here we go. We are actually doing this. This is crazy. Crazier than running a mile home in front of a car? Yeah, I think so. My dad speeds ahead, Mako and I follow, still crying. At the side of the hill, there is a church with a fence surrounding it. Each time we run up, we take cover behind the fence before running back down again. My dad knows we're doing this but seems to accept it. Maybe he realises how hard it is just to make it to the fence.

Every step up the hill is hell. Every step down is treacherous. The wind, rain, sleet and snow are as relentless as the hill is steep. But we persevere in the dark. We have no choice anyway.

There is never a point where I think that this is OK, and we're going to do it, or it's not actually that bad. That never happens. It's a continuous procession of misery and pain. I try to focus on just getting it done, with each step knowing that I am a tiny bit closer to the cosy warmth of our house. At least I'm with Mako, we can help each other. But it doesn't help. I still have to do it.

We make it up and down five times. Then six times, then seven. I know it's nearly done. But that still doesn't make the next time any easier. It's actually harder because I'm exhausted. Because about half-an-hour ago I was watching wrestling with Mako and was not prepared for this in any way.

I think about The Rock as we make it eight times. What would he do? He'd give my dad The People's Elbow. I wonder if it would hurt my old man?

I think it's getting colder. I can feel it actually turning far colder than *it was when we came out here. We've barely broken a sweat because it's so cold. This might be dangerous. I don't know why, but it feels like it might be.*

We've done it nine times and this is now the last time up and down. Once again, that doesn't help. It's harder than any of the previous nine. I think of The Rock. I think of elbows. I think of warmth.

And now it's over. With the help of that fence, it's over. My dad has powered through double the amount in the same time as we did our repeats. It's over. At last, it's over.

● ● ●

We're back indoors to find that welcoming cosy warmth. A place where an eight-year-old and a ten-year-old should be, on a night like this.

My dad is talking to us, explaining why he did something so crazy, so terrifying and so traumatic that I will never forget it for the rest of my life.

'Guys, I want you to focus on school, not rugby,' he says.

'What's he talking about?' I think. 'I love rugby. This doesn't seem to make any sense. Do I want to be a rugby player if I have to do this?'

'If you want to choose rugby, this is what you have to go through,' he tells us. He should know, he is a rugby player.

'Why don't you just sit down in the warmth, with a cup of tea and revise school work instead? It's so much easier than rugby with all that running and getting hurt. And you won't have to worry about the security of your next contract and feeding your families when you're grown up.'

My dad's motivations are clear. He wants us to choose the safe bet.

And he's right. What he's saying makes so much sense. But sense doesn't matter with something like this.

I want to be a rugby player. He's way too late. We are already hooked. We never miss training. We have a rugby ball in our hands most of the time, day and night. We are going to be rugby players. We know it and he knows it.

● ● ●

In actual fact, my dad's brutal plan to scare us off from focusing on rugby had quite the opposite effect. He forced us to make a choice at a very young age and we emphatically chose rugby. So we ran and we ran and we ran. And then we ran some more. We hated it, but it didn't matter because we had chosen rugby. We had been offered an alternative but we signed up for the oval ball, and we did as we were told because my dad knew what he was doing. Those ridiculous hill sprints in the snow were a major turning point. They still motivate me to this day and remind me of what I had to go through to move up the rugby ladder. They also make me think of the sacrifices my family made for us to help realise our dreams. My dad put up with so much.

He didn't realise it then, but coping with the awful weather and alien surroundings of his new home in South Wales when he first arrived on his own in 1998 was already part of our story. His plan at that time was to stay for a couple of months, play professional rugby for Pontypool, then return home to Tonga and take his whole family to Sydney, Australia, where he had a scholarship place waiting for him to study for his Masters degree in building economics. Sydney over Pontypool? It seemed like a solid plan to me.

But life is unpredictable – this was the first time my dad had ever been paid to play rugby. Back home, he'd represented and captained our country and relished the honour, but the attraction for him was that rugby was a hobby, something to go alongside his profession as a quantity surveyor. It was also a way to see the world, and playing for Tonga had taken him to the places he wanted to see, including South Africa.

After that South African tour, my old man was one of ten Tongans who were offered representation by Phil Kingsley-Jones, the agent of All Black god Jonah Lomu, who had arranged the trip and brought over Lomu's people to help Tonga develop as a rugby nation. As well as being the most famous rugby player in history, the late great Lomu was of Tongan extraction which was to prove hugely influential in the path of our family, because around a year later, Kingsley-Jones set up the deal for my dad to come over to Britain and play for Pontypool. At the time, he was thirty-two and coming to the end of his career, but there was a World Cup in the UK around the corner and, as it was a country he had always wanted to see, he opted to pop over and play for a bit. But he was almost denied entry to the UK, thanks to his persistent honesty.

Dad received his contract from his agent, but not his work permit. He was sent a plane ticket and told he could come into the UK as a visitor from Tonga, so all would be fine. He boarded the plane, flew 10,000 miles and went back thirteen hours in time only to find that British Customs officials wanted a word with him. Being a truthful man, my dad answered their question of why he had come to their country by explaining that he was here to play rugby.

'Have you got a visa?' they asked.

'I don't need a visa,' he replied, incorrectly.

'No, you don't need a visa as a visitor, but if you are here to play rugby then you must have a visa.'

'I'm sorry, I don't have one.'

'Well, in that case, you're going back to Tonga.'

'Well, in that case, it doesn't matter. I'm here because I wanted to have a look around the country but now I know that you're not nice people, I want to go back!'

This took the Customs officials by surprise: 'Is that right?'

'I came all the way, I wanted to see Great Britain, but now I'll go back and take my family to Australia.'

'Are you sure? You said you came here to play rugby and now you want to go back?'

'I do want to play rugby, but I don't have the visa. My agent is outside and I think he's got my work permit.'

'Do you have his number?'

'Yeah.'

At this point, Customs called Phil Kingsley-Jones, who was waiting in the airport to meet my dad, he handed over my dad's work permit, and he was then allowed to stay. The first Vunipola to set foot in Britain.

'You're the first man who came here and said he wants to go back!' laughed the Customs official as my dad entered the country.

'Well, I didn't know you were going to be this rude!'

'No, we were doing our job.' And they were right.

Apart from UK Customs and Jonah Lomu, my late grandfather Sione also played a pretty significant part in our journey to the UK. He was also a rugby player in his spare time, and turned out for Tonga against the All Blacks in the 1970s, when he wasn't being a policeman back home. He had a dream. Not like a Martin Luther King dream, but a fairly big dream all the same, which was for us to relocate to the UK because of the opportunities that awaited us there. He never got to see me and Mako pull on England shirts, but I know how proud he would've been and I'm sure he's watching our every move. But we might only have been putting England shirts on ourselves as fans, had my dad not listened to Sione.

In the first instance, before most of us had even visited the UK, it was my dad's dad who had practically pushed us the thousands of miles over there. While my dad was struggling in Pontypool, Sione was preaching in our church and announced in front of the entire congregation that we would all be joining my dad over in Wales. Well, that was news to us! But it worked. It was all anyone from the church could talk about, and it quickly became a fact. We were soon on our way.

Sione was at it again a few years later, when we'd all returned to Tonga for a holiday which dad was planning on making permanent. At that point, Dad had had enough of the UK. He'd had to fight so hard for every rugby contract with Pontypool and subsequently Pontypridd. My mum wasn't working, my dad was sending money back to his parents in Tonga and it was a struggle for him to make ends meet. Life back in Tonga would've been so much easier for him. He would've had a comfortable lifestyle with a good job waiting for him, a house and a mortgage. What more could he have wanted?

'It's a hard life there, I'm coming to the end of my career and I feel like giving up,' Dad told Sione one day. 'I want to stay here and practice as a quantity surveyor.' Sione never said a word. Later that night, when we had our family prayer gathering, Sione said he had been surprised by what Dad had said about returning to Tonga permanently. And the words he spoke then, were words that would stay with my dad for the rest of his life. When my dad recalled them to me years later, he had tears in his eyes.

'If I was given the opportunity to raise my family in Great Britain in my lifetime, I would fight tooth and nail to do so,' said Sione. 'This is the chance of a lifetime for an ordinary Tongan. The only Tongans who have the opportunity to even visit the UK are the royal family or government ministers. You have this chance, so you must struggle and you must fight, because I know you have it in you to do this for your children.'

It was the moment that changed everything. From that point on, whatever my dad did was going to be for his dad and for us. Our trip back to Tonga would remain as just a holiday, because we were heading back to Britain for the rest of our lives.

2

Broccoli for Breakfast

I'm standing around on a rugby pitch, watching the game go by again. I can see the ball. It's roughly two miles away on the other side of the pitch. There's no way in hell I'm moving my butt to get that thing. If it comes near me, great. I'll do something. I don't know what, but I'll make something up. Whatever comes naturally.

It's pretty cold. I'm not used to this. Where I come from, it's not like this. It's not like this at all. Where I come from, you can wear shorts every day. I used to wear shorts every day. I still do in the house, but not outside. Except now.

I'd better move around a bit to keep warm, the ball's a bit closer now so you never know. I think we're losing the match. It's hard to know exactly what's going on.

'Hey Bill,' I hear.

'Bill!'

I turn to my right and one of my uncles is yelling my name. He's got his hand next to his mouth as if he's making some kind of megaphone to amplify his voice. What does he want?

'If you score three tries, I'll take you to McDonald's!' he shouts.

There's a bit of laughter around him, and a few more looks in my direction. This is not a decision that will take me more than one second to make.

'Sweet!' I say.

He's smiling.

I'm smiling.

'Gimme that ball right now,' I think as I look down the field to see what's going on. And what's going on is that my brother's involved in something. He's winning the ball. Yes! I'm getting closer now. I'm right in the thick of it and, before I know it, I somehow have the ball. Other kids, older than me, are throwing themselves at me.

But they can't stop me. I'm massive. I'm massive and I'm playing in a game for kids who are two or three years older than me. They're older than me and I'm running through them like they're not there. But they must be there, because I've dumped some of them on the floor as I run.

I'm thinking about McDonald's as I put the ball down over the try line, and there's a little cheer from my team-mates and a bit of noise from the sidelines too.

OK, let's do this.

From the kick off, I'm chasing that ball. I'm chasing that ball like a kid who's never had a McDonald's before. And I almost am that kid. I've only ever had it once. And that one time is the best thing that's happened to me.

The best thing ever. Better than getting on a plane and coming to the UK. McDonald's. Goodness me.

I've got the ball again, and I'm charging forward. Someone's trying to hang off my leg, but I'm not having it. Nobody is stopping me and this ball. We are one. I run in another try. 'That's two down, one to go,' I think to myself as I trot back to my half. There's noise coming from those watching, but I can't really hear it. I can't really hear anything, because I'm focusing on just two things. The ball and the Big Mac.

We're playing again. I can't get the ball. I need that ball, but I can't get it. Someone from the other team still has it. I try to get, it but the ball's gone.

Keep moving. Stay hungry. Literally. It's not as easy as it was before.

Keep moving. Stay hungry. The other team still have the ball.

Keep moving. Stay hungry. The ball's on the ground. The ball's on the ground. The ball's on the ground. I can reach it. I can get it. I have it.

Keep moving. Stay hungry.

I'm running. There's nobody near me. I'm running towards the posts. I'm going to score again. I've scored. That's the third one. Job done. McDonald's here I come. Focus on the Big Mac. Keep moving. Stay hungry.

I think we're winning. It doesn't matter anyway. I'm winning.

I'm walking around again and the ball is nowhere near me. But it's OK. I'm winning.

'Hey Bill!' calls my uncle again. 'Score another one!'

What does he mean?

'Nah,' I say. 'You already said three for McDonald's. I'm done.'

My uncle is laughing. He's laughing hard. I'm smiling too. I'm winning. I carry on walking. More tries are scored but not by our team.

The game is over now and we've lost. Except me. I'm winning. I'm going to McDonald's.

● ● ●

I loved McDonald's. I loved it like a kid who unconditionally loves his family. To me, McDonald's was the place where I was happiest. It was home. Except I didn't get to go there that often. A couple of weeks before my uncle set me that challenge, my dad had taken us all for a McDonald's one evening. He didn't want my mum to cook and it probably seemed like an easy option. He was right. We all loved it. But I wanted more, and I didn't realise an opportunity for a return trip would come so soon after.

My uncle actually tried to get out of it. I'm not sure if he was just kidding, but he must have seen how serious I was about going there, because he soon stopped joking around about reneging on the deal.

The truth is, I loved my food. And I still do, although I eat a little bit differently these days. Back then, as a kid living in Caerleon, Wales, and turning out for Newport High School Old Boys on the pitch that was just behind our house, I didn't have to worry too much about nutrition regimes, my weight, and things like broccoli and kale. Hell, I wouldn't have even known what those vegetables were at that time.

I grew up in a culture that was based around food. Everything we did revolved around eating. And when we ate, we ate together in a joyous way. We celebrated food, and the beauty of eating and enjoying food together. Any single event was an excuse to feast.

Take Sundays for example. Back home in Tonga, Sundays are all about church and eating. It's a beautiful thing.

In New Zealand, they have the traditional Maori way of cooking which is called a Hangi. The food's cooked in a pit oven, which is dug in the ground and heated stones are then placed in the pit with a large fire. Baskets of food are placed on top of the stones before everything is covered with earth for hours and hours. We do a very similar version except ours is called the Umu, and that's how we cooked our pig every Sunday. My mouth is watering just thinking about it.

We also put the hot rocks from the fire which cooks the pig into a pit that's dug in the ground and then all the food goes on top of the rocks. The food is then covered by earth, blankets and pillows to make sure all the heat is kept in. Every single Sunday it's the same drill, and it never gets boring because that pig tastes good.

That was how it was, and how it still is, as we brought those traditions over to this country. To me, eating was always a joy and I loved to eat everything I could. I was a big kid. When I say I was big, I don't just mean I was tall, because I was at least a head and shoulders bigger than almost everyone my age and most kids one, two or three years older than me. I also mean that I was large all over my body. The truth is, I was an overweight child. I don't know the technical definitions, but someone today may have described me back then as obese.

But it was never a problem for me. I didn't eat well, but I loved my food. And because I loved my food, I didn't eat well. It never really hampered me either, I was still able to play rugby effectively. Obviously, if I'd have shed a few pounds, I would've been a more effective player which is exactly what happened to me much later on in my career. But, as a kid, it just wasn't a significant problem. And it never occurred to me that it was a problem. That's how much it wasn't a problem.

School dinners definitely didn't help all that, but what an extraordinary treat they were. Me and my boys still talk about them to this very day. During the 1999 World Cup, we had the best lunches and I don't mean the slops that were dished up in the canteen. I'm talking about the amazing feasts that were cooked by my mum, and Josh and Toby's mum, as we were all living together during the tournament. First thing in the morning, they'd be going for it in the kitchen in a massive way by frying up chicken nuggets and chips for us, while we were tucking into breakfast. Then, at lunchtime at school, while the other kids were scoffing their sandwiches, Freddo Frogs and Penguins, me, Mako, Josh and Toby Faletau would be trying to scrounge some ketchup as we delightedly wolfed down our nuggets and fries.

As I got older, and my appetite became increasingly insatiable, the nuggets weren't cutting it for me. When I went to the Castle School after we moved to Bristol, once or twice I would turn up to school with a whole chicken in my bag. Seriously. An entire chicken, one of those beauties you can get from Tesco. And when I was hungry, I'd just dip my hand into my bag and devour a leg or a bit of breast. It was awesome, until my teacher Lloyd Spacey caught me chomping on a wing and gave me a strange look. I'd spend the whole day snacking on that bird, while other kids would be eating their Mars bars or whatever. I couldn't have been happier.

Not that I had anything against Mars bars. Chocolate was actually a massive weakness for me and it still is. I absolutely loved the stuff, but I have to make sacrifices these days. Time was, as long as I had a cup of tea to help wash it down, I would nail one of those monster, family-size bars of Cadbury's Dairy Milk. The amazing thing is, if I didn't eat chocolate for a while, I wouldn't miss it. But as soon as I tasted it, I would have another one, then another one. And then suddenly I'd have ended up having four bars of chocolate. Sometimes I might have felt a bit low and I'd think, 'Well, one bar of chocolate won't hurt,' and I could end up having one, or I could just as easily end up having six.

Christmas was brilliant in addition to the usual stuff, because we'd get one of those flat selection packs of chocolate with all the Cadbury's greats in them. I'm sure someone used to nick mine though, because when I'd go to my box with all the enthusiasm of a wide-eyed kid seeing their first Christmas tree, I'd be gutted to find that the only chocolates left were a Chomp and a Fudge which nobody liked. Whoever it was might have been doing me a favour though, because that kind of lifestyle, exemplified by the extra large kebabs Josh and I would always indulge in whenever we went to Marmaris, our favourite Pontypool kebab shop, meant that I wasn't getting any lighter.

We loved going to Marmaris, it was a kebab institution for us. We worked up a racket where we would stand around on the streets near Josh's place then intercept anyone we knew who was heading into the house.

'Hey! Got a fiver on you?' we'd ask every single person. 'We just want to get a kebab.' If we asked enough of them, a few might drop us a fiver, we'd get kebabs and might also be quids in. The only problem was when they asked each other, 'Hey, did Josh and Billy ask you for a fiver?' and we were rumbled.

With the extra large kebabs on top of the rest of my diet, by the time I turned pro with Wasps, I was absolutely enormous. As a professional rugby player, I'm weighed very often so there are no hiding places because those scales do not lie. I'm not kidding but I think there might have been a time when I was around 150kg. That's more than twenty-three stone which is insane. That was my first year out of school, and Wasps made it clear the fat had to go.

I was trying my best to lose weight, but I still didn't know how to eat properly. I hadn't been properly educated about food, so I wasn't aware that stuff like crackers, yam and cassava were all carbohydrates that were heavily starched. I didn't think it was that bad because that's what we grew up on, so I carried on eating the same things but I was training twice as hard.

I was doing fat burner sessions where you do half an hour on the bike before you've eaten anything in the hope that your body will burn fat for energy. I started snacking on banana and milk in between smaller meals, so I was trying to eat more regularly which is a good thing – smaller portions and more often. Wasps had given me a training programme. And it worked. In just three or four weeks, I got rid of about 14kg.

But I was getting carried away with it. I kept thinking, 'Right, I need to smash this and keep getting the weight off.' So, instead of eating properly, on my days off from training, I was just chowing down on banana and milk every three hours. I know it sounds crazy now, but it made sense to me at the time. If I kept having banana and milk, the weight would come off, I told myself. I was barely eating anything else. Occasionally, I was so starving that I'd have to eat some meat and vegetables for dinner – that was the only luxury I would afford myself. I was stupid, but when you get caught up in something like that, you honestly think you're doing the right thing. But I was wrong. In the end, my body just buckled and gave up.

● ● ●

I'm feeling so ill. I don't think I've ever felt this ill. I know everyone says that when they get ill, because they forget what being really ill is like, but this isn't just that. I actually feel so awful. I've got the shakes. Actual shaking, all over my body. Shivering, shaking and sweating. I can't stop these cold sweats. I just want it to stop. And my back is killing me. Have I mentioned that? My lower back is so sore.

But I have to get control of this. This is not how I've been taught to handle this kind of thing. I've been brought up to be tough and to never acknowledge that I'm in any pain. Man up. Tough it out. I can get through this. I need to fight.

My back is hurting so much. I make a hot water bottle. This will sort me out. A hot water bottle always sorts me out.

I sit down on the chair in front of the TV and place the hot water bottle in between my back and the chair.

I lean back.

Wow! That's hot. That's so hot. I don't think the sun could be much hotter than that. But I'm ill. That's probably why it feels so hot. It feels like it's burning me. I can get through this. I just need to tough it out.

I put the TV on. It's distracting me from the burning, although the burning still burns. Because that's what burning does.

All in all, this is not too bad – this feels a bit better.

I can't focus on the TV. I'm drifting. I think I'm falling asleep. I must be falling asleep. I just need to tough this out.

●　●　●

What the hell is that?

I'm awake.

What is that on my back? It's killing me. Oh crap. My back is hurting even more than before. I peel the hot water bottle off my back and inspect it.

Something isn't right. There's no cover on it. Just the latex. There never was a cover on it. Just the burning rubber. Burning my back. Blistering it. Skinning it. Shredding it.

Oh my gosh. No wonder. The pain. The burning. Everything.

I don't know how long I've been asleep, but the damage has been done. If I needed to tough this out before I fell asleep, now I really need to tough this out. But I'll be fine. I'm in great shape, my weight's down. I'll be fine. Tomorrow is another day.

●　●　●

Tomorrow is here. It's today. And it's absolutely no different from yester-day. I'm freezing-my-balls-off-cold. I'm sweating and shivering at the same time. Something isn't right. I know that something isn't right. But I've got to get on with it. I've got to. I can get through this. I just need to tough it out. I'll be fine. I'm in the car with my dad, who can see something's up with me but he doesn't say anything. We're on the way to the Wasps training ground in Acton. They'll sort me out. They know what's good for me. They know what I need.

We're at Wasps. I'm still shaking and freezing. The physio is looking at me with a concerned face. Eventually, he says, 'You look ill.' That much I already know. 'Go and get checked out,' is his advice which I take.

So now I'm in the car with my dad again, heading all the way back to High Wycombe. To the hospital to be precise, to A&E. Time to find out what the hell's going on. Because even though I can tough this one out, and I'm going to be fine, I might as well see what a doctor thinks about it all.

My back is now more painful than I can ever remember anything being. Even getting hit with a broom handle by my mum would be preferable to this. And now, not only is my back killing me more and more as each second passes, but this is all happening in public, in the waiting area of the hospital casualty unit.

It's called a waiting area for a good reason. Because since I got here about three hours ago, all I've done is sit around waiting. Sit around waiting while in pain. It's so frustrating. Both the pain and the waiting. I can feel myself becoming increasingly agitated.

How can I be made to wait like this? How can any human be treated this way? I know I need to tough this one out, but I just can't do it anymore.

My dad's trying to calm me down as he can sense my mood is changing. But it's no use.

I'm crying. I'm bawling my eyes out. I'm sobbing in the middle of the hospital, in front of everyone.

'Are these guys taking the piss?' I protest. 'I'm dying here and no-one's trying to help me out!'

People are staring at me. I try to wipe the tears away. This is a low. I know it can't get any worse than this. And I'm right.

● ● ●

Turns out that you can't really tough out pneumonia. Who knew?

What's more, you can't really tough out discitis, a serious back infection.

By the time I got into my hospital bed at about one in the morning, I was in a lot less pain but I knew I had a long way to go to get better. I'd let myself get into a bit of a state in my obsession to lose weight. Ending up in hospital was definitely not part of the plan.

Ward 6C at Wycombe Hospital is always fresh in my mind as a place where I learned so much about myself, and about how the world works. From the discomfort of my window bed on which I couldn't lie down due to the state of my back, I could see the incredible work done by the doctors, nurses, physios, porters and all the dedicated staff, who looked after me for the four weeks I had to stay there. They were amazing, and it wasn't long before I was regretting my outburst in A&E. I just had no idea how busy and overstretched these places are which was why I had to wait for so long.

While I was on the ward, I couldn't walk around because I had to rest due to the pneumonia, so the porters used to push me everywhere. I got on really well with them and we used to hang out together – it would have been a different experience without them.

Not only could I not sleep on my back, but I also couldn't lie on my side as my shoulders were so sore from training. That, and the IV needle they put in my hand kept catching on my wrist, so they had to do a little operational procedure on me which saw them fit the needle into my bicep. I wasn't too bothered about that, as long as the thing stayed in.

During that time, when I wasn't trying to catch up on sleep or watch TV, I had plenty of visitors. My brother Mako came to see me and I could see him walking through the corridor clutching a bag of KFC – that brought a smile to my face because I couldn't ever recall him doing anything for me before. He sat himself on the seat next to my bed, didn't really say much, and then just chomped down half of the chicken himself before I interrupted his munching jaws by saying, 'You bought that for me, you idiot!'

He handed over the goods and it felt good to eat some junk food like that after everything I'd been through. I'd fallen right off that particular wagon.

Despite that, there were some days in hospital where I didn't feel like eating anything at all. I just wasn't hungry. It was a peculiar feeling, because that has never happened to me at any time in my life either before or after. I remember being on my bed thinking how I wasn't feeling even slightly peckish. I smiled to myself and thought, 'This is cool!'

Other visitors included my England Under-18 coaches Peter Walton and John Fletcher, and the manager Charlotte Gibbons, who all travelled a long way to see how I was doing which was amazing and showed me how much they cared. And, of course, my parents were there the whole time. Not that my mum went easy on me. She had her own unique theory about why this had happened to me.

'Billy, everything happens for a reason. Maybe you're just too arrogant?'

'Mum, give me a break!'

'Look, you're even answering me back in your sick bed.'

'Yeah, because I feel like I'm gonna die!'

'I just think you need to be humble.'

It sounds harsh, believe me, I get that. But you need to understand our relationship. My mum always has a gauge on why things happen in life. And she's usually right too. I wouldn't be here right now as an England rugby player without the guidance of my parents. What my mum's view taught me was that I had got a bit too big for my own boots. I had got carried away after making my pro rugby debut while still at school, and maybe I needed this experience to bring me back down to earth. There were things in life that were more important than rugby. Like treating people around me with love and respect all the time. That whole experience gave me a new focus.

But not before I switched hospitals. After a month in Wycombe, I was transferred to Stoke Mandeville as that's the top place for back injuries. It was emotional to leave Wycombe – the nurses didn't want me to go – but it was for the best. After a fortnight in my new surroundings I was done and it was time to swap the institution of the NHS for the institution of Wasps rugby. It was going to be a long way back after six weeks out, but I was approaching it with a completely different attitude.

Bananas and milk was off the menu forever. I knew my diet was important, but it wasn't the be-all and end-all. And neither was rugby. I just wanted to have fun and enjoy life, which was nothing new for me, it was just a case of re-ordering my priorities.

Despite my new outlook on life, food and everything, I still struggled with my eating for a long time afterwards. Let's make one thing clear. I never struggled with not eating enough; that was never going to be a problem for me. It was much more about what I was eating and when I was eating it.

They say old habits die hard, and that was exactly the case with me and my diet. My old Wales Schools coach Dawson Jones likes to tell a story that Mako and I used to devour whole saucepans of potatoes back when we were kids. That's because we would eat whatever was available and easy. We could cover the potatoes in mayonnaise or something and that was a decent snack to keep us going.

My parents didn't know any better when it came to our nutrition regimes. In fact, they wouldn't know what a nutrition regime was then or now. Their main concern was to keep us fed so that we didn't go hungry. And they never let us down on that part. Despite all that, my dad still had a six-pack in his playing days, even with what he ate. But Mako and I were fed up to be massive and fat and we had to spend many years just trying to burn that fat and put some muscle on. As a result, my brother was terrible at running and that's why he ended up as a prop. And the big man still loves to eat, to be fair.

It was only really in the time after I joined Saracens that I started to get the hang of eating right and cutting out all the junk. And even then, it took a while. I was never aware of how picking at food can add up. Until very recently, I would watch TV accompanied by a variety of snacks like cake, biscuits or chocolate and drinking Coke to wash them all down. I wouldn't even be aware of how much food I was eating, as I'd be consuming it over a long period of time and would never feel full from snacks like that.

I was also extremely stubborn from a cultural point of view. People from my background do not eat salad. It's just not a thing for us. So I would refuse to ever tuck into anything like that.

In my old days of eating, I would often wake up in the morning and skip breakfast. I'd then give myself permission to have something like chicken and chips for lunch, because I hadn't had breakfast, so it was fine to eat that. Even then, it wasn't just chicken and chips for lunch. It was an extra large portion of chips, sitting alongside a whole chicken. Obviously.

I would then usually be much too full to even contemplate eating anything else until around nine in the evening, by which time real hunger would have set in, and I'd be caning more huge portions again. This time, instead of cooking at home, I might treat myself by going to the kebab shop and getting something like a chicken shish. The key to it was to eat whatever came easiest. It's hard to believe now, but I just didn't know any better.

These days, things are very different. Once I started to get the hang of it, the changes came quite quickly and naturally. I was helped by my girlfriend Simmone who is a dietician and taught me loads about eating properly. She made me more aware that you can train as hard as you want, but if you're not eating the right stuff you're not going to lose weight. It's a simple equation that if you're burning more than you're eating then you're going to lose weight.

She also taught me the basics. I had no idea that eating too much bread was bad for you. I also didn't know that consuming too many carbs is fine if you're exercising and planning on burning them, but a bit of a problem if not. Without that exercise, those carbs will turn to fat. This was all new to me and learning key information like that made me more aware of exactly what I was eating every day and when I was eating it.

Simmone also made me understand how to eat consistently. Instead of skipping meals and making up for it later, it was crucial to have breakfast, lunch and dinner equally spaced out throughout the day. And snacking was also encouraged but what I snacked on was key, so I'd replace slices of toast with a healthy yogurt. It wasn't just food that needed to be consistent, my sleeping patterns also came under scrutiny – building sleep around all the meals completed my whole new routine. It was really automated and kind of robotic. And it sounds really boring. The truth is, it *was* really boring, but it helped to get me where I needed to be.

These days, I always have breakfast and lunch at the training ground which makes life much easier. I'll go there straight away in the morning and have a slice of toast with four eggs, baked beans and some broccoli too. Yes, I even have broccoli for breakfast. I'll look at it and think, 'What the hell am I doing?' but I know that it makes me feel good and reinforces that my hard work is paying off.

After training, if it's been a tough session my lunch might be something like rice, mince, more broccoli and green beans, which is another thing I would never have eaten before. In fact, my meals have generally become a lot more colourful in recent times. I might have an afternoon snack at about 4pm – I have a fruit bowl at home these days – then dinner at about 7pm and that's it for the day. I'm also more careful on days off. If I'm not training, I won't down four eggs when I can just have some Weetabix and toast instead.

There are always fresh challenges though. My aunties regularly treat me by sending over cakes and other sweet stuff which I can never say no to, because I don't want to be rude. So I always say thank you, give myself a little treat, then invite the boys over and make sure they polish it all off. At Saracens, there are no hiding places when it comes to weight – we have to hit the scales every morning and they also test our fat percentage. It's the best thing for me as it keeps me focused. And I can see that everyone faces different challenges when it comes to eating right. People like my team-mates George Kruis and Jackson Wray have to eat about 14 times a day just to keep on their weight otherwise their body just burns it naturally. That's tough for them, because they just don't enjoy eating that much. And I look at them and think to myself, 'I would love to have that problem!'

Sometimes, though, you do have to feed the soul. Even though I'm now a healthy eating evangelist, in the back of my mind, I know I'm still a junk food freak at heart, and I can't restrict myself forever. After my first game for Saracens following a three-month knee injury in 2017, I was straight on the fish and chips.

You have to have a balance with everything in life and I guess I came through that tough experience to get to the place where I am right now. I made myself a promise when I came out of hospital and that was to never deprive myself again. If I feel like I am doing that, then I'll stop immediately because depriving myself made me ill and I never want to feel like that again.

The fact is I do love my food and I always will. It's part of who I am. I'm sure that by the time I'm done with rugby, I'll probably be fairly overweight again. In fact, I'm one hundred per cent certain that I'll be overweight when I'm done with rugby. And I'm looking forward to it!

3

Wrecking Ball Jr

There's a big man talking to us about PE. He's very tall, must be around six and a half foot at least and broad with it.

He's talking about sport in school, rugby, that kind of thing. I'm staring at him. So are loads of other kids sitting alongside me in the big, main hall at the Castle School in Bristol. And he's staring right back at us.

It's our first day here so, for once, we're all in this together. I haven't been thrown in the deep end and started right in the middle which is what happened in Wales.

But Bristol is very new to me. It's different to village life in Wales. The school is bigger. The city is bigger. The people are friendly but they speak weirdly.

I'm sitting three rows from the front with the rest of my form. It's called 7G.

All this talk is a bit boring though. Even if it is about sport, which I like. I *prefer to actually play it. Well, rugby anyway. I don't know about the other stuff that the big man is banging on about.*

I'm fidgeting, feeling restless. I look around the hall. There are all sorts of kids in different shapes and sizes. Boys and girls, it's a mixed school. Big ones, little ones, fat ones, thin ones, tall ones, short ones, pretty ones, ugly ones, wide ones and narrow ones.

And me.

I'm way bigger than every other kid in Year Seven. And probably Years Eight and Nine too, but they're not in the hall right now. I'm even bigger than a number of the teachers who come to talk to us this morning.

Right now, I'm sitting down. But on my two feet, I'm six foot. I haven't weighed myself for an age, but I must be around 110kg, or seventeen stone now. Even on my chair, I'm still pretty big. Are other kids staring at me? I'm sure they are. I'm certainly staring at them, so why shouldn't they return the compliment?

This is so boring. When do we go to a classroom to actually learn something?

When's lunchtime? When's school done for the day? Actually, I'm not so fussed about that because Dad wants us to run after school today. Man, I hate that.

What's going on? Everyone's getting up, I think we're done. Yes! Hang on, the big man's walking towards me. He's got his eyes fixed on me. Gosh, in trouble on my first day – that's probably a record, even for me.

'What's your name?' he asks, towering over me like the giant from Jack and the Beanstalk.

'Billy,' I reply, not in the most enthusiastic way. I'm on the back foot here,

and I don't even know why, so I fix him a glare and give him the bare minimum in terms of response and body language.

'You obviously play rugby, do you?'

No shit, Sherlock. I'm not exactly a jockey, am I?

Fortunately, that's what I think, not what I say. What I actually say is an even more defiant, 'Yeah.'

'Well, that's interesting. We've got rugby training on Thursday so I'll see you then.'

'Yeah,' I reply, still in the same manner.

And he walks off.

Well, that went well.

I have no idea why I was on the back foot. I guess I was just standing my ground. Anyway, come Thursday, I'll show him what I'm all about. I'm now really looking forward to that.

● ● ●

It's Thursday and there are around seventy of us doing drills, messing around with the ball on the school rugby pitch. This is fun.

I have a ball in my hands and I'm spinning out passes that are travelling twenty or thirty metres at a time. Other kids are looking at me in amazement.

'How do you do that?' someone asks.

I shrug my shoulders. I don't know how I do it. I've always done it. I've always had a rugby ball in my hands so I just do it.

It's like me asking you how you breathe, right? You just do it.

The big man from the other day is here – his name is Lloyd Spacey and he's running the session. He's already said hello to me, and I grunted something back at him. For no reason.

We split into groups to practise rucking. Great, I love this. It's easy and it's fun.

Spacey is holding the tackle pads and kids are running into him, dropping down to the floor and then laying the ball back – exactly as you might do in a game.

Everyone's lined up and one by one, they run about ten metres, crash into Spacey's pads and place the ball down.

It's my turn after the next guy. I need to make a good impression and show him what I can do. I'm ready to go. I'm excited. I don't know what that feeling is, but it's running through my body. It's anticipation. It's adrenaline. It's crazy.

I'm off and running towards Spacey.

He's getting closer.

The pads are getting closer.

I'm going quite fast.

I've only got about ten metres to cover but I'm trying to sprint into the pads.

I hit the pads hard.

I hit Spacey hard.

His whole body flies up into the air and he lands with a thud on his back.

I hit the deck and place the ball down.

Job done.

'Not bad, Billy,' he says with a wry grin on his face, as he springs back to his feet.

'I'll hit you harder next time!' I reply. Because I can't help myself.

● ● ●

Sensibly for both Lloyd Spacey and myself, we didn't go for seconds that afternoon. There was really no need. The truth is that when I was eleven, I had no idea about the power of my own strength. Luckily, the people in a position of responsibility knew all about it and, for safety reasons, I would often play with Mako in teams that were two or three years older than my age group. It wouldn't have been a good idea for me to be hitting other kids my age given how much bigger and stronger I was than them.

Not that it always helped with the safety side of things, because I had previous when it came to flattening people.

A couple of years earlier, during a training session with the East Wales Schools Under-11 squad, I managed to break the ribs of Ross Williams. These things happen, you may well say. But the problem was that Ross wasn't one of my Welsh school team-mates, he was a grown man who also happened to be the chairman of Pontypool and District Schools Rugby. Oops.

Even at the age of six, pretty much from when I first arrived in the UK and started playing rugby in Wales, I was always way bigger than every-one else so played with older kids. It was usually just easier for me to play with Mako. Although back then, they were playing a kind of rugby that was completely alien to me.

Having arrived from Tonga, I was used to playing a contact game. We weren't violent people, but we didn't know any other way to play rugby.

There *is* no other way to play rugby. Except when I got to Wales, I found out there was.

On that pitch behind our little house in Caerleon, I made my debut on these shores for Newport High School Old Boys. It was memorable for all the wrong reasons as I didn't quite get the hang of the key rule of the game which was described to me as 'touch' rugby. For the uninitiated, as I so clearly was back then, touch rugby is the same as normal rugby but instead of tackling and full physical contact, you just touch the opponent to make them stop. Yeah, right.

So in my first game, while all the other kids were playing nicely and touching each other and saying things like, 'Would you mind awfully if I could have the ball now please old chap?' – OK, I made that bit up – I was just flying into tackles all over the pitch, making other kids wince and cry, much to the concern of everyone watching, and to the great amusement of my family on the sidelines.

I didn't find it that funny. I wanted to play rugby, but instead I had to stand around in the middle of the pitch watching other smaller, more nimble and faster kids run rings around me as they could catch me easily every time.

I remember thinking, 'I hate this game', and muttering to myself about why the hell we were playing touch rugby. And when I became frustrated, it was to hell with touching, and time for me to introduce tackles and hand-offs into the game. You know those YouTube videos you see with that one massive kid bombing it across the pitch, pushing everyone off him and leaving a trail of destruction in his wake? That was me.

Looking back now, it's obviously funny but I was annoyed then as it didn't make sense to me. Fortunately, within a few weeks it was no longer a problem as I progressed to full contact rugby, playing with Mako, Toby, and the older kids. That was more like it.

I was always going to stand out as such a large child – even playing with the older kids, I was still absolutely massive. It was common for coaches and parents from opposing teams to query my age. Nobody believed I could possibly be the age I was. Kit was a problem as well. It wasn't just that my dad was struggling with work which meant I had to make do with whatever battered old gear was lying around, but it was also very hard to find kit that actually fitted me. Especially when I had to wear a particular team's colours. At the Castle School, I managed to struggle through with one rugby shirt for around three years, I was the only kid who ever borrowed the teacher's boots to play as Lloyd Spacey's size thirteen-and-a-halfs were perfect for me, while it proved utterly impossible to ever find a suitable pair of rugby socks. Instead, I either wore white ankle socks, or no socks at all.

It was a similar story with school uniform and it became the bane of my mum's life trying to keep me kitted out with the regulation gear as I kept growing. Although it was her side of the family that I have to thank for my size, so fair's fair. My mum and her family are all tall and naturally broad people and she's actually way taller than my dad.

Even though I knew I was bigger than everyone else in my class at school, I can honestly say it was never a major issue for me. Everyone was used to having me around, although it did mean some special arrangements had to be made. All the kids had tables to sit at in the classrooms with trays that you could pull out underneath them and matching low chairs to perch on. The furniture was the right size for all the kids, but way too low for me. I simply could not fit around any of it.

A solution was found in the shape of a shelving unit which had loads of pull-out trays in it. They just ripped those trays out and, with the help of a normal-sized chair, I was able to place my feet underneath the unit and concentrate on my schoolwork. The only problem was that because of the size and shape of my large desk I couldn't sit with the other kids, so I was placed on my own right next to the whiteboard. I had to see the funny side of it, because that was the only way of putting up with sitting like that throughout Years Four, Five and Six in school – it was only in my secondary school where the furniture was a size that could do a better job of accommodating me.

Back on the pitch, my size was starting to dictate where I would play. Even though I could spin those passes and nail drop goals from anywhere within about twenty-five metres, I was big and I carried a whole load of chubbiness to go with everything else I brought to the party. So it wasn't long before I was playing prop. My dad wasn't happy with that, and neither was I really.

Prop is one of the hardest positions to play and I didn't think it was right for me – even at a young age, I knew it wasn't my best position. Technically, it's a tough role to fill in open play, because you're one of the bigger lads and everyone around you is smaller and faster than you. For me, it was like being back in one of those touch rugby games again. Also, being in the scrum puts a lot of pressure on the shoulders, way more pressure than I'd have if I was playing number eight as props take the full force of the scrum.

Because you have to take all that weight, you have to be heavier – and then everyone expects you to do everything else on top of that. I was never any good at the scrums, and it's possible I didn't want to be good at them.

It's a far more demanding position to play prop in aerobic terms as well. I was always more comfortable with doing all the good-looking stuff like running with the ball and making all the big hits. Essentially, everything that's associated with a number eight now, although these days everyone's trying to get the prop that does everything.

In our district schools team, I was prop alongside Mako, who was the hooker until I got to about eleven, and then I started playing at eight but I wasn't very good. All I had going for me was my size, as I didn't understand what to do with the ball, or how to use it effectively. But my team-mates always gave me the ball anyway, because that seemed to be the general game plan: give it to the big bloke.

Despite being a big kid, when I was young I was always really scared of getting hurt on the rugby pitch. Playing alongside Mako and Toby was a real education for me. They threw themselves into tackles, ran amok on the pitch, side-stepping opponents and scoring brilliant tries. They were probably ten or eleven and I was seven or eight, but I was in awe of what they were doing – they just weren't afraid of getting hurt. And I was. People might have looked at me then and seen a little beast, but the truth is I was not that tough. I'd look at the other two and think, 'Why can't I be more like them?' and occasionally I'd surprise myself by just running from the halfway line, hoping for the best, and scoring a try. But if I wanted to be who I wanted to be, I really should have been doing that the whole time, rather than being a bit soft and worrying about taking a few hits.

Getting hurt wasn't the only hang up I had.

● ● ●

The sky is looking so threatening and menacing, it's almost as if I can sense something bad is going to happen. It's so dark, yet it's daytime and it's not raining. It's just moody and eerie, and I feel scared.

Where is this place? Where the hell are we? It's like we've entered the gates of hell to play a school rugby match. Even the people here look like extras from a horror film. I'm so scared. I'm just a nine-year-old kid far away from home.

I stay close to Mako. He's older than me and he's not scared. If I'm near him, I'll be OK.

We have our kit on and we're on the pitch ready to play. But it's not really a pitch. It's a field. Like a boggy bath of mud. There are no lines on it, just posts at each end. That's the only way of knowing that we're here to play rugby.

I think back to this morning, when I had no idea I was going to be playing until I got to school and the coach asked me to turn out for the Under-11s. I was chuffed. I still am, but this place is seriously creepy.

● ● ●

We're playing, Mako is getting stuck in, and I'm trying to run around a lot but I'm just getting really muddy. The mud is everywhere. I think it's on my face, but I can't tell. I've never seen mud like this, it's like biblical mud, if there is such a thing. It's hard to see the colour of the kit which I had to scrape together from school Lost Property because the mud has splashed all over it. It's the same for both teams, there's just a load of muddy kids stomping around in a field.

We're winning easily, when I get the ball on the halfway line. I decide to run with it. 'If you can't beat them, join them,' I think, after seeing Mako and Toby do this often enough. I almost want to close my eyes and hope for the best, because I don't think I'm going to like getting tackled in this mud bath, but that would be a bit daft.

I'm moving quickly now, two players have tried and failed to take me down. I'm heading to the posts. There's another challenge, then another, but I'm past them both and I touch down before I've even had time to really think about what's happened and how I did it.

As I get up, I hear myself saying out loud 'Wow! Did I just do that?'

'Shut up, you big-headed idiot,' says Mako, who's standing a few feet away from me looking unimpressed.

Sometimes, I surprise myself.

The sky is even darker. I can't think of a worse place to have done something like this.

● ● ●

I'm standing in the corner of the changing room and I'm crying. I'm so scared and ashamed. I don't know what to do.

The game's over, we won. But now I'm covered in mud and I don't have anything to change into. My school clothes are back in my school. I didn't know I was playing until this morning, that's why I wore Lost Property kit for the game.

But I'm not even crying because of that.

What I'm crying about is much worse.

All around me, eleven-year-old boys are getting their muddied-brown shirts off and walking around in their pants, as if it's perfectly normal.

I don't know where to look.

Where I come from, we don't do this. We have privacy.

This lack of privacy is humiliating. For me and everyone here. I can't stand it. It makes me feel uncomfortable and uneasy.

I'm a big lad. I don't want everyone to see my belly. My belly is my business, not anyone else's. I am ashamed of it in these kinds of surroundings. If I take my top off, I expose myself, pure and simple. And I don't want to do that.

On top of all that, these boys are all much older than me and used to this kind of thing. I'm only nine.

After all this time, I'm still sobbing.

I'm still standing in the corner of the changing room.

And I'm still frozen with fear when Mako notices me and my state.

He walks over, and looks at me with the most sympathetic face I'll ever see on him. Or am I wrong and he's just going to smack me around the head for crying like a baby?

'What's wrong?' he asks me, looking concerned.

I'm right about him.

'I don't have any clothes!'

'Stop crying! Just take your clothes off.'

'No, I don't wanna show anyone my belly and I'm not taking my pants off in here.'

'Are you being serious?'

I nod, trying to stop crying.

'Are you crying about that? Here, take my clothes.'

With that, Mako gives me his change of clean clothes, and returns to his spot in the changing room. My humiliation is spared by my brother as I somehow squeeze into his clothes without giving anyone a glimpse of my flesh.

He is my hero.

He now emerges from the changing room wearing a black bin bag over his filthy rugby kit, which he has to sit in for the whole journey back home.

I'm too young to fully appreciate the gesture. But, even so, I know he'll never do anything like this again.

● ● ●

These days, Mako barely says a word to me. But sparing my blushes remains the most loving thing he's ever done for me. It's tough to over-estimate just how petrified I was of the embarrassment of showing everyone my body. It wasn't something that came naturally to me, because I didn't think that was the way people should be around each other. I was just a kid with childish hang-ups. It wasn't just that I was ashamed of my big belly, but I was culturally alienated by the communal way everyone got changed before and after sport in the UK, with everything proudly on show. I couldn't have been the only kid to have issues with that.

Fortunately, as I grew up, my anxiety about that whole thing diminished. I realised that British society is less judgemental than Tongan culture. Perhaps what I was afraid of was how back home, everyone gets ridiculed for the way they look. In Tonga, they are savage about your looks and there's nowhere to hide. If you're fat, everyone will tell you that to your face. And if you're skinny, they'll also tell you to your face that you need to eat more. Over there, so many people are overweight that nobody has a problem with pointing it out.

Once I understood that wasn't going to happen here, I felt more comfortable about being undressed in front of others. There was never a scenario where someone would point at me and say, 'Gosh, he's a bit fat, isn't he?'

I was also helped by the fact that there were way bigger people than me who I was sharing changing rooms with. When I saw the state of their bodies, my attitude was, 'Oh, if he can do it, then I can definitely do it,' so I just became far more comfortable in that sort of environment.

I was always comfortable on the pitch too, despite the occasional mud bath that cropped up here and there. By the age of eleven, I was playing district rugby for Gwent and then East Wales Schools – while trying not to break the ribs of any more of their officials – and I remember that being the time when I became convinced I could make it as a pro one day. It actually coincided with our move away from Wales, over the Severn Bridge to Bristol, where my mum got a new job as a minister of a church in Thornbury where we would live. That was when I really started loving the game as well. We were playing on Sundays, and everything just felt a bit more real and serious.

At that age, it was possible for me to do ridiculous things on a rugby pitch. In one game, for the Castle School against Clifton College in the Daily Mail Cup, I think I went over the line four times, nailed all the conversions and added a couple of drop goals as well just for fun. I'm not writing this to show off. I'm just trying to explain how much fun I had back then when I was allowed to do that on a rugby pitch for the joy of just playing. There was absolutely no pressure. What was particularly enjoyable about it was noting the attitude of the Clifton College kids, who paid good money to go to that school, before the game. They turned up with a certain look about them and the odd comment along the lines of 'we're gonna smash this lot', so playing a part in making them eat that attitude was satisfying.

The result, and my performance, even made it into the local Thornbury newspaper with the headline 'King of the Castle'. I found that extremely embarrassing, even more so when my mum's friend would repeat the headline to me every time I saw her. Finally, after one more 'It's the King of the Castle!' from her than I could take, I snapped: 'That was two months ago and we lost in the next round so just drop it!'

In another game for Castle, we were struggling to make any impact, so our coach Lloyd Spacey moved me to fly-half and the match situation quickly changed for the better. Suddenly, I was running the backs line. Good times.

I played for Bristol Schools but I heard that there were questions raised about whether it would be safe for the other kids for me to play in the same games as them. That's not me being big-headed, that was just because I was so much bigger than everyone else. I could also move fairly quickly for someone my size, and those two things combined meant it might be fairly serious for someone half my size to get in my way. I know I certainly wouldn't have been happy if the situation was reversed. And I'm sure I would have questioned the age of anyone my size and build if I was a parent or coach watching on the sidelines, like so many did with me.

Lloyd had plenty of faith in me and he made me captain from the out-set, and I would always try to repay that faith by helping out with the organisational side of things, like sorting out all the kit, and helping with practice sessions. I think despite my occasional surliness – I was a teen-ager after all – Lloyd could see how much I cared about my rugby and he knew I would never let him down. Together, our school teams won loads of cups and tournaments which was a great feeling.

Space would always wind me up by saying, 'You're going to play for Wales one day,' but I'd shoot him back a look and say, 'Nah mate, Australia or England.' In theory, all three were possible, as I was born in Sydney because my mum travelled there specially to give birth, but I hadn't even turned pro yet so didn't want to get too carried away. Once Mako and I were playing in the county system in England though, our decision was made. At that point, we had our hearts and minds fixed on playing for our new country one day, no matter what Space or anyone else might have said. Even though it was still years away, it was always in the back of my mind.

Sometimes, it was hard not to lose focus and think too far ahead, as the level of interest in me and my rugby started to grow. As much as I played it all down and stayed humble, it was impossible not to think to the future and dream about what might lie ahead for me on a rugby pitch.

By the time I got to fourteen or fifteen, I was getting offers from schools with amazing sporting reputations like Millfield and Bryanston and that's when I really knew I had to start taking everything even more seriously and try to push on as much as I could.

There was a tournament at Millfield which Castle School qualified for by doing well in our region, and we nearly went and won it. People there had barely heard of our school and we almost won this competition, so people sat up and took notice. Afterwards, a guy called John Mallett who was in charge of rugby at the school talked to Lloyd, a mate of his, about me and asked the usual questions about my age, my real age and that kind of thing. At the time I was in Year Nine, but Mallett was looking for someone older who could join the school for sixth form, so he asked Lloyd if I had any siblings.

'Well, his older brother Mako is in Year Eleven,' said Lloyd.

'Is he as good as his little brother?' asked the Millfield man.

'He's better.'

Lloyd was right. Mako is better than me, but I'll always say to him that if it wasn't for my performance in that tournament at Millfield, he would never have gone to that school. So, let's not beat around the bush, I got Mako his scholarship!

As good as that experience at Millfield was, for me personally, Rosslyn Park was probably a more significant tournament in terms of recognition and making a bigger impact. It was a nationwide schools tournament that I played in when I was in Year Ten, and I'm pretty sure we beat Eton that day. I have no idea how our tiny school ended up involved, as it's a tournament that you have to be invited into to play, but we must have been doing something right. I wasn't really aware of this but Space told me afterwards that during one of our pool games, London Irish came out to train on one of the adjacent pitches to where we were playing. While our game was going on, one of the London Irish lads called Topsy Ojo came to speak to Lloyd.

He tapped him on the shoulder and said, 'Are you with the Castle School?'

'Yes,' said Lloyd.

Ojo then signalled towards me on the pitch with his eyes and said, 'Who the hell is that?'

After Lloyd had explained who I was, Ojo disappeared before returning with a load of his team-mates, supposedly to watch me play, which was weird to hear about afterwards. A while later, my dad received a phone call from someone at London Irish but nothing came of it. Nothing apart from me realising that I was in demand, and although that increased the expectation, I tried to stay laid back and humble. My default mode.

● ● ●

BOOM!

Mako steams in to me, and sends me flying and landing with a thud on the muddy grass.

'Idiot!' I yell at him.

BOOM!

He's on top of me now. He's laying into me. Our fists are flying into each other and we wrestle on the ground. He's angry. I wind him up some more. He gets angrier. And so it goes on. I can't hit him back though, because that's not in the rules. I can protect myself from his blows, but as he's my older brother I have to show respect for the pounding he's trying to give me and not reply in kind.

So I cover up and take the worst he's got. I can handle it.

Eventually, Toby and Josh break it up so we can get on with the two-on-two garden rugby game. It's the usual teams: Me and Josh v Mako and Toby, who insisted on wearing some new shoulder pads we'd just got. Or Good v Evil, as I like to call it. You can win the argument to wear the shoulder pads, Toby. We'll win the game.

We're in the Faletaus' backyard in Pontypool where we always hang out, playing rugby or just being kids and annoying the hell out of each other.

The two-on-two is competitive. We don't go easy on each other and that's how it should be. I get on really well with Josh, we're similar characters. Mako and Toby are also alike in that they're quieter types. Two perfect pairs to make two tough teams.

But we shouldn't even be playing today. Not today. It's Sunday. Toby and Josh's dad had to go out to work, but he has left us strict instructions.

'It's Sunday so don't play rugby. Please clean the house then just chill,' he said before he left.

So here we are in the garden playing a sometimes brutal, overly-physical game of rugby. It's nice and chilled. But if you look in the house, it's definitely clean. You could eat your food off the floor, it's so clean. That is the part of the bargain we have kept.

We scrubbed that place from top to bottom and it was all done in about ten minutes. There is no way that Mr Faletau is going to know whether we played rugby or not, we all reason. As long as the house is clean then we're good to go. And so we do go. Out into the garden to play rugby. What's the worst that can happen?

Time to get on with the game.

Never mind respect, I'll teach Mako a lesson on the pitch. He's got the ball, but I can't get close enough to him. He lays it off to Toby, and I'm run-ning towards him from behind. He can't see me coming.

But right now, I bet he can feel and hear me as I land right on top of him, sending him crashing to the ground. That's a good hit.

'Aaaaggghhhhhh!'

That was a very good hit. Toby doesn't normally cry out in pain like that.

'My shoulder! Aaaaggghhhhhh!'

Wow, it must be the timing. I didn't even realise it was that special.

'Aaaaggghhhhhh!'

OK, this has gone far enough. I want to play more rugby, and so do Josh and Mako who are standing with hands on hips waiting to get on with the game.

'Come on Tobe, stop messing around,' says Josh.

'Aaaaggghhhhhh!'

He's definitely joking. One of us always does this kind of thing until the others take it seriously and then we mock them for believing us. Seen and done it hundreds of times.

'Very funny, Tobe,' says Josh. 'Let's get on with it.'

'Aaaaggghhhhhh, my shoulder!'

Enough is enough. We never usually go on with the charade for this long, so Toby is really starting to wind me up now. Josh and Mako are not looking very impressed either.

I crouch down beside Toby.

He's hunched over and I can see proper pain on his face. Are there even some tears there or is that dew from the grass? Either way, I'm starting to worry. I'm starting to think he's not messing around.

I touch his shoulder.

'Aaaaggghhhhhh!'

'Oh crap,' I think to myself. 'He's actually being serious!'

'Guys,' I say to Josh and Mako. 'He's hurt.'

All those times when we mess around with each other, feigning injury, laughing and joking around, winding each other up. All those times, but now it's actually happened. Toby is actually hurt. And, wouldn't you know it, it's me who's hurt him by smashing through the back of him.

'Sorry, Tobe,' I offer. 'I didn't mean to . . .'

There's not much I can say. He looks in a bad way.

Josh tries to help him up, but the screams get worse.

'I've got to call my dad,' he says.

Great. He couldn't have been at work for more than about twenty-five minutes and now he's coming home. More to the point, now he's going to know we did the exact opposite of what he asked us not to do on a Sunday. Even more to the point, now he's going to find out that I seem to have seriously injured his son. Crap.

At least the house is clean.

● ● ●

I'm not sure Mr Faletau really took in how spotless the house was when he rushed back in to see what had happened to Toby. Shame, really. For some reason, he was far more concerned with the welfare of his son, who it turned out had properly busted his shoulder. Correction, it turned out that I had properly busted his shoulder. He had a dislocated collarbone – those shoulder pads hadn't really done their job – which meant he was out of rugby for what must have seemed like a lifetime to him.

It certainly seemed that long to me, especially feeling somewhat responsible for what happened and, although he never said it, I'm sure he was probably annoyed with me. I definitely would have been annoyed with him if the roles were reversed.

It was a delicate time for Toby because I think he came close to giving up on rugby when he was struggling to recover from the injury. As a kid, it's really hard to come back from an injury like that and go on to play rugby again. You're young so you don't really think injuries through and have a plan for rehab like you do when you're an adult and in the hands of a professional club.

Fortunately, he did make it back on to the rugby pitch and we even resumed the odd game of two-on-two garden rugby, but I would never hit him like that again. Even when we became pros, the first time we played against each other, I found it difficult and couldn't really smash into him in the same way I would anyone else in an opposition shirt. The emotions were confusing. Here's a guy who's practically family, who I shared so much of my childhood with, and now I need to hurt him? I found that hard to deal with and the first time we met as pros when I was playing for Wasps and Toby was lining up for Newport Gwent Dragons, I kind of wrapped him up instead of absolutely smashing him whenever we went head to head. It got easier as I became more used to that kind of thing happening over the coming years, but given the choice I would much prefer the option of having Toby as a team-mate. That's a lot less painful.

Playing with Toby on my team reminds me of some of my best rugby days when, alongside Mako and Josh and our cousin Anthony Maka, we all played for Bristol Colts. It was a glorious time. Just imagine the look on the opposition faces every week when our team turned up, coached by my dad, with five more burly Tongan lads forming a third of the starting XV. We had a really strong team, and I played whenever I could even though I was only fifteen and the others were at least seventeen. I was still bigger than most of the opposition though and I used my size to great advantage, even managing to channel my inner Jonah Lomu when my dad put me out on the wing.

They would chuck the ball to me and more often than not I'd run like hell and somehow score a load of tries. It was good, but I couldn't keep that up. I wish I played wing now, but those boys are a different breed these days. And they're all good looking, fast and fit.

Back then, the joy of speeding down those vast empty spaces near the sidelines was immense. Anyone coming within a metre of me would get the hand off, or a cheeky side step. I knew there were people watching nearby who were chuckling away as I tore it up and, to be honest, I did get a buzz out of that. Who wouldn't?

But my presence on the pitch also drew a lot of complaints. Once, I played against a team called Chew Valley. I was out on the wing again and scored three or four tries. Some guy on our team called over to me, 'Mate, how are you doing that? You're only fifteen years old!'

One of the Chew Valley players heard and then decided to complain, saying I shouldn't be playing because I was too young.

He was right because I was still an Under-16 and according to RFU rules, I wasn't allowed to play Under-18 rugby. But Bristol managed to get special dispensation for me to play because of my size, arguing that it wouldn't have been safe for me to play with other guys my age because I could've caused injuries. We had to send a photograph to the RFU of me standing alongside a nineteen-year-old, showing I was the same size or even bigger.

Then there was also frustration from our opponents which boiled over into racism, given that a third of our team was Tongan. We beat everyone that season, but some of them took it badly and there was abuse. That's just the way it is. We're in someone else's country pissing about, and winning, so it was obviously going to annoy some people. But you just have to get on with it, although it used to annoy me when I was younger. I'd get in loads of arguments over comments that were usually about the colour of my skin. 'Mate, shut up!' would be my standard response.

I now understand that that kind of thing is always going to be there, lingering. No matter how much we want it to change, I don't think it will so we just have to deal with it. Just be kind to as many people as you can, that's the best way to treat it. Otherwise, you waste your energy.

Despite the odd problem like that, I only really allow myself to have beautiful and happy memories of those great days in the Colts. Under my dad's stewardship, we became South Gloucestershire champions, but it wasn't just about winning. It was about the joy of playing alongside all my boys. Our gang. Together like that, and winning.

It was just so awesome. We all still talk about it now. We'd just bounce off each other, and talk to each other on the pitch in Tongan, saying things like, 'Mate, bang him! Bang him!' or 'Alright, I'm gonna have a run now!'

It would be the last time it happened, as things got serious for some of us shortly after that and we all started to go our separate ways. But it was a fitting way to end an innocent time. A time where we could play without pressure or expectation. A time where we could play with smiles on our faces, and just enjoy the feeling of working hard for each other, and having a good laugh about the game afterwards. It's probably that same feeling that loads of guys up and down the country get every weekend when they turn out for their local league teams with their mates. It's a beautiful feeling that should be cherished. And I really miss it. Of course, I miss that.

But playing for Saracens and England is not a bad substitute.

4

Pie and Crash

I'm holding down a struggling, young boy.

I'm feeling so weird and scared.

I'm not the only one pinning him to the floor.

There are four or five of us.

He's struggling and panicking and trying to break free from our grips.

But it's of little use as he has no chance.

This is awful. I don't understand why I'm doing it, but I have to because the teacher has asked us to do it. What can I do?

If I don't, I might be in the position of that boy before long.

From behind me, the teacher approaches wielding a large branch of a tree and carrying a very stern look on her face.

I've no idea what's about to happen other than it looks like it's going to be painful. Is this really the right way to discipline a ten-year-old kid? He keeps running away from school and forcing him to the ground seems to be the only way to make sure he stays put.

The teacher is now standing near the boy's feet and raises the branch backwards in the air, high above the boy.

I hold my breath.

I don't know if the boy is also holding his breath, but I can see the fear in his eyes. He's absolutely bricking it. So am I.

I notice that the rest of the pupils fixing him down are looking in the opposite direction. They've probably experienced traditional Tongan education before, as have I, but I've still not seen anything quite like this spectacle.

These thoughts continue to flood into my head as the teacher swings the branch from up high and brings it crashing down to slam firmly into the soles of the boy's feet.

He yells.

I wince.

He yells more. It's a scream of fear, as well as pain. A scream of the unknown and of terror. A scream I can hear even after the last of it emerges from the back of his throat.

I can't look. I can't watch this anymore. I can barely even hold him, but I don't have to try too hard now as he seems resigned to his fate and has stopped trying to wriggle away.

I'm not looking anymore, but I'm still aware what's happening and it isn't pleasant. The branch comes down on the kid's feet again.

And again.

And again.

Even if he wanted to run away from school again, there's no way he could do that now.

Is that the idea? Hang on, that's the idea!

As the penny drops, so does the branch once more on to the boy's feet.

'Please don't do that again,' I think to myself.

I can't imagine what this poor boy must be thinking. Probably the exact same thing, to be fair. The kids holding him directly opposite me suddenly let go and I look up, not understanding what's happening anymore.

It's over. It's over.

I let go too.

The boy stays on the floor and immediately grabs hold of his feet which just look really red from what I can see. But it's hard to see because he's clinging on to them really tight, and he's not going to let go anytime soon.

The poor kid.

I feel so bad for him.

I'd feel bad for him anyway, but I'm like an accomplice to this whole thing.

I know this is not my fault, but I feel like this is definitely my fault.

But it isn't. This is just a normal occurrence.

This is Tonga.

● ● ●

At this point, if I was to try to convince you that my country has a totally laid-back vibe about it, you'd laugh me all the way to the loony bin. But you need to go with me on this one. Tonga may still believe in corporal punishment at school and in the home, but that isn't the beginning and end of its traditions. My country is old school for better and for worse. When you've been stuck in the middle of the South Pacific Ocean for all those years, old habits die hard.

School in Tonga was very set in its ways. Apart from the way justice was meted out in a terrifying manner, we all had to wear traditional Tongan clothes for secondary school. So I used to wear a ta'ovala, which was like a mat that you put around your waist, and a tupenu which is a garment that's similar to a sarong and is worn by boys and men. The thin material trails down to your calf and is wrapped around the waist.

Despite the fact that I only turned up to school when we returned home for the summer, I still never received any special treatment. Which means that when punishments were dished out for not doing homework, which I never did because I was only there temporarily, I would have to join a line of kids waiting to be whacked. Someone was ordered outside to break a branch from a tree, while we had to remove the ta'ovala because otherwise it would have broken any branch that swung towards it.

We then had to accept a whack on our behinds which would prevent us from sitting down for some time afterwards. Not only that, but it was also not possible for us to show that we were hurt. Displaying any signs of weakness or pain were absolutely forbidden or your classmates would be given license to mock you mercilessly.

Looking back on it now, that was an extremely scary experience for me to have to go through. Yes, I was used to receiving hidings from my parents, but to have a complete stranger whacking my butt with a branch from a tree took some getting used to. Obviously that kind of thing would have been completely unacceptable back at my school in the UK, but kids in Tongan schools were far better behaved than any of the schools I went to here. I'm not saying that justifies it, but that was just my experience. Every time I returned to Wales after a spell in Tonga, I would never really discuss those kinds of things with my schoolfriends. I didn't think they'd be interested and I didn't think they'd believe those kinds of wild stories either.

Tonga is made up of more than 170 small islands and they are beautiful. The average island is certainly not average. There's nothing average about it whatsoever. In fact, most of the islands boast white sandy beaches, coral reefs and tropical rainforest. Lagoons and limestone cliffs are ever present on my home island of Tongatapu where it never gets cold, or too hot. It's perfect, it's idyllic and it's where I'm from.

The Vunipolas come from a small village called Longo Longo. When I say small, I mean it would take less than a minute to drive through it. But you wouldn't drive through it. Because you wouldn't need to. Back home, we don't bother driving through the village. We don't even bother walking through it. If we want to get somewhere, we go the shortest possible route – even if that means walking straight through other people's houses.

Everything in the village is more or less connected so you could be sitting at home minding your own business in front of the TV, when somebody would just stroll straight past you, say 'Hey, how are you?' and then just carry on their way out of the other side of your house. And the really funny thing is that you wouldn't even look away from the television. Because that's business as usual.

It's way quicker to get somewhere by walking through our neighbours' homes than it is to go the long way round. And nobody's got a problem with that. Growing up, there was a rugby pitch about 100 metres away from our house. Well, it was 100 metres away assuming we were going to walk straight through two villagers' houses. Which is exactly what we always did. A couple of quick, 'Hey, how are yous?' and we'd be right on the pitch ready to roll. Although, the chances are that nobody else would be. Because even though our social conventions made it as easy as possible for us to get anywhere, our laid-back genes made it almost impossible for us to arrive anywhere on time. In Tonga, it's widely accepted that on time means not even close to the specified time. If we were supposed to be on that rugby pitch for a training session at 3.30pm, there is no way in the world that the action would begin until around 4.30pm. It just wouldn't happen. Obviously, the guys who organised the rugby in our village weren't that bothered about the time. In fact, I know for certain that they weren't because our local village team, Toa Ko Maafu, has been run by Vunipolas since Sione was in charge of it.

I remember so many times, when I was a young kid, my mum and dad coming home to see how we were getting on after school, and telling us they were just popping in because they had a big meeting to go to in twenty minutes. An hour later, they'd still be with us, chatting about the day, having a second or third cup of tea and not in any particular rush to go anywhere.

To say that England is the total opposite would be the understatement of the century. Probably the biggest wake-up call that any islander has faced when adjusting to life in the UK is the fact that everything doesn't just happen on time, it happens early. You need to be some-where before the scheduled start time so that you're actually ready for the start.

I know that kind of attitude would draw laughter in Tonga, but we're all different. Heck, if you saw some of the cars that people drive around in back home, you'd also crack up laughing. I mean some of those heaps of metal are seriously unsafe. It's not uncommon to see people driving cars with doors hanging off their hinges, or without any doors at all. And there they go, cruising down the road like it's no big deal. And with a speed limit of 40mph because everything is so close together, maybe it isn't such a big deal.

Life is very different in Tonga because it's so deeply rooted in the past. I'm not saying it's a third world country, but the attitudes are third world as old cultures dominate life. Not that that's a bad thing. It's what I love about Tonga. Even if you were to go to the relatively under-developed nearby nations like Fiji or Samoa, they'd still make Tonga look like you'd just stepped into a time machine and gone back a century.

Take Sundays in Tonga, for example. Everyone goes to church in the morning and I mean everyone. The only people who don't are those responsible for cooking the Umu I talked about when I was telling you how much I love to eat. Because everyone's going to church, it was always fun as you'd see friends and family. As kids, we'd have a sleep after church and then it was time to feast. Once we'd given the food our best shot, we would all go to an absolutely packed Sunday School where we'd learn more about our faith, before it was time to eat again. Every week, Sundays were simple yet extraordinarily special days.

Another old Tongan tradition is the kava ceremony, in which adults gather together to drink the kava plant extract. My dad was always a big fan. It's not alcoholic, but it's the customary way many people in Tonga, and other Pacific islands, will sit together and socialise. You get the drink by pounding the roots of the kava plant into a powder and then adding water and pouring the whole mixture through a sieve. It has kind of a sedative effect in that it can make you calm, more sociable and slightly numb your mouth. I liked it, not because I ever drank it, but because when my dad was drinking kava, I knew it was a time to be free, to hang out with my cousins, cruise the streets or whatever. We also did that in Pontypool, where my dad would drink kava with his islander mates. Once we'd moved to Bristol, I hated it though. That was because he'd always be feeling sleepy when we were driving back from Wales, so he'd have all the windows in the car wide open to keep him awake. We would absolutely freeze our faces off sitting in the back of the car, yet somehow we could fall asleep in the middle of all that. I always remember the point where we would have arrived back in Thornbury and my dad woke us up. We'd be frozen solid every time.

Life in Tonga was pretty sweet. We were fairly spoilt because my mum and dad had good jobs. My dad was a quantity surveyor, and my mum was an accountant. When they were busy working, my grandparents took care of us which was awesome because they let us get away with murder compared to my parents. Generally speaking, there were a lot less hidings, a lot less running and a lot more weight added to our bellies. Often, we'd get back to the UK after a summer in Tonga and my dad would absolutely smash Mako and I with running because we'd larded up so much while we'd been away. Getting back was definitely the worst part of being away.

● ● ●

I'm staring at a house.

It's a very simple picture of a house. One of those flash cards you see in school which you're supposed to recognise in a flash. Hey, maybe that's why they call them flash cards?

That's cool.

But anyway . . .

I am in a new school and I do recognise the house picture.

The only problem is I just can't say what it is out loud.

And I have no idea why.

In my head, I'm saying 'house, house, house, house, house'.

But that's no help because nobody in the room can hear what I'm saying in my head. Which is unhelpful right now, but probably quite helpful for the rest of the time.

I look around the room for help.

I turn to my grandma, she smiles at me.

She has no idea that I'm going to completely mess this up. Why would she?

I'm her blue-eyed boy, so to speak.

I can't do anything wrong.

I certainly can't fail this simple test to get me into this brilliant English-speaking free school for the summer, can I?

House, house, house.

It's all I can think and all I can't say.

House, house, house.

The teacher sitting opposite me, holding the card with the house on it, smiles at me.

I'm not smiling back.

I'm a bit scared.

I don't really know what's going on with my head and my mouth and why they're not talking to each other.

House, house, house.

The teacher looks at grandma.

Grandma looks at me and smiles.

'Come on, Billy,' she says. 'Tell the teacher what it is.'

But I can't. I just can't.

I look at my grandma with confusion in my eyes. She looks at me, for the first time with a slight sense of disappointment. It's not a look I've seen her give me before. I want to change that look.

House, house, house.

But I can't.

'Come on, Billy!' I say to myself. This isn't hard. Tongan kids who don't speak English could do this. I have the advantage of speaking English and spending time in the UK.

But, for some reason, I can't say it.

The teacher decides on a change of tact as she produces another card in place of the house. It's a chicken. It's clearly a chicken. There is absolutely no doubt. If it looks like a chicken, the chances are that it's a chicken.

'Chicken,' I say.

But that word doesn't come out of my mouth. There's no sound at all.

I say it in my head. I can say it in my head as many times as I want.

Chicken, chicken, chicken.

But I just can't say it out loud.

Chicken, chicken, chicken.

I can't do it. Why can't I do it?

Chicken, chicken, chicken.

Grandma looks at me again.

This time, she's really quite serious, although she tries to smile to cover it up.

It doesn't help.

The teacher still looks encouragingly at me.

It doesn't help either.

Neither my grandma, the teacher or the chicken can help me.

Chicken, chicken, chicken.

When is this going to end?

How will this end?

Chicken, chicken, chicken.

I don't know when it will end, but it's not going to end well.

How will the school accept me if I don't know how to say what these pictures are in English? Even though I know them, they don't know that I know them.

Chicken, chicken, chicken.

This is driving me crazy.

The teacher looks like she's really nice. She has a nice voice and face. She smiles a lot.

Grandma isn't smiling so much now.

'Come on, Billy!' Grandma says again.

'Stop saying that and help me,' I think to myself.

Chicken, chicken, chicken.

'Do you know what that is?' Grandma asks me in English.

'Yes!' I think. 'Of course I know what that is. It's a chicken. Everyone knows it's a chicken. Except I can't say it for some reason.'

All the time I'm thinking this, I'm staring at Grandma, waiting for her to help me. To say the word for me.

Chicken, chicken, chicken.

'Come on, Grandma,' I think. 'Help me!'

Chicken, chicken, chicken.

The teacher has had enough of houses and chickens.

'Can you spell dog?' she asks me.

That wouldn't be an easy question for a kid from Tonga, whose first language is not English. But I know how to spell dog. I've been to school in Wales, I know how to spell dog. It's D-O-G. That's how you spell dog.

But knowing it is one thing. Saying it is another altogether.

D-O-G.

Grandma's staring at me now. She's staring at me so hard that it hurts.

The teacher is staring at me too. She's staring at me with a smile. But, somehow, it also hurts.

Time is standing still.

D-O-G.

Nothing can save me. Not even my grandma.

D-O-G.

I'm thinking that Mako passed this test easily. Mako is coming to this school and I am not because I can't speak.

D-O-G.

I can feel Grandma's disappointment. I can feel the teacher's disappointment. But the feeling I can feel most of all now is my own disappointment.

D-O-G.

Why is this happening?

I have no idea.

But I know that I'm going to be paying for it.

● ● ●

We called that school the Tonga side school, because it was on the side of the bigger Tonga High School, and was the place you went before progressing to the senior school. That was just what you did. It was what everyone did. But not me. Because I'm not everyone.

I was like a rabbit caught in the headlights during that interview. I completely froze and that was bad news for my parents and bad news for me. The side school wouldn't have cost them a penny, but they now had to send me to a fee-paying school instead. When my dad asked me what had happened during the interview, I told him that I couldn't answer any of the questions because I was too shy to say the answers in front of my grandma. That explanation was my one-way ticket to another hiding. So it was bad news all round.

To top it all off, Tongan radio then announced that I hadn't managed to make it into the side school. Their story angle wasn't that a future international rugby player had flunked his school interview. It was because the traditions in Tonga are so old school, that they actually announce on the radio whether kids have made it into the school or not. They don't bother sending out letters, making telephone calls or anything like that; you just have to tune in to the wireless to find out!

Once I'd overcome that particular humiliation, it was time for me to go to the school that would accept me for who I was, rather than the side school that intimidated me so much that it stopped me from speaking. That's my version of the story anyway.

The school was called Ocean of Light and I loved it. But my passion for the place wasn't really down to educational reasons. It was purely a life-style thing. The day would start early at 7am. Yeah, I know. Once I'd got over that shock to the system, I'd get involved with a bit of play and learning, or whatever we were supposed to be doing, until it was time for lunch which they served to us late morning because we'd started so early. Lunch there was amazing. It was the highlight of my day. I can still taste the incredible steak and kidney pies that I'd have almost every day. It definitely wasn't the healthiest meal they could've given us, but at the age of six or seven that wasn't really a priority for me. Those pies were my priority and when I say pies, I really do mean pies plural, because once I'd destroyed whatever had been put on my plate, I would then polish off all the pies that the other kids had criminally wasted.

Then after lunch, like manna from heaven, one of the teachers would say, 'Get your mats out, it's time to go to sleep.' Nap time was an extraordinary luxury. I can't imagine that happening in Wales. There was no time for sleeping there, we had too much work to do. In Tonga, I had time to eat my lunch, everyone else's lunch and then have a long sleep. Nap time was supposed to be an hour, but I must have been experiencing some kind of carb slump, because I would often sleep all the way until 3pm when school ended. The teachers would wake me up and say, 'Billy, it's time to go home,' and the first thing I would think as I opened my eyes was, 'Yes! How good is school?'

It was only a summer of living that particular life but it was a glorious summer. Well, it was until I got busted. One day, Sione came to pick me up from school. All the other kids sprinted out to whoever was collecting them, full of the joys of a good day at school. But there was no sign of me. Sione was confused and wondered where on earth I was, until the teacher came out to speak to him.

'He's still sleeping,' explained the teacher.

Sione started laughing. He was chuckling away as he came in to wake me up, and he kept laughing all the way home. There were my parents paying all that money for me to go to the school, and there was me sleeping the day away. The smile was still on his face when my dad turned up from work and Sione announced, 'Billy is living the high life!'

'What do you mean?' said Dad.

'He's been sleeping off half the day. He's only going to school for half the week!' said my grandad, trying to suppress the laughter that was still there in the deepest recesses of his throat, waiting to go off again.

My dad looked at me. Not that I could see it that close-up, but I think there was anger coming out of every pore of skin on his face. And it was all directed at me. I couldn't read his mind but I knew what he was thinking then and I certainly know what he was thinking now. It was the usual story – I was the little devil who was spending his days sleeping and acting up like an idiot, while my parents were working hard and my brother was in the best Tongan school being an angel every day. It was the story of my early life. And I didn't do anything to help that situation improve. In fact, so many of the things I did just made it worse.

It all stemmed from the time when I was a baby and my parents left me to go to New Zealand. Even though I don't remember it, because I was only a few months old, my dad thinks my dodgy behaviour as a kid can be traced back to that time when my grandparents looked after me for more than a year while Mako went to New Zealand with my parents, who had to finish off their studies.

They were on scholarships but money was tight and they felt that bringing me with them as a five-month-old baby would have been too expensive as they couldn't afford a babysitter for me. Mako was old enough to go to a nursery school so he was covered. It was a major sacrifice for them to make, and I know that they regret it now but at the time they thought they were doing the right thing.

Not that staying with my grandparents was a bad thing. It was great. They spoiled me rotten and I became quite attached to them, so it was no surprise that difficulties followed when my parents and Mako returned. I don't think it's possible for a kid of that age to be separated from their parents and for it not to affect them both immediately after they return and also long term. I'm no psychiatrist, but it's a classic case of separation and attachment theory. I'm a textbook example, which helps explain so much of my subsequent behaviour as a kid. And if that sounds like an excuse, it is one – hell, if I'm being offered one, I'll take it.

So many of those very early memories are very hazy as I was so young, but I know from my parents and grandparents that I was a whole heap of trouble from the moment my family returned from New Zealand. We were all living under one roof – my grandparents' roof – so it became very hard for my mum and dad to impose themselves as parents again, because I had firmly attached myself to my grandparents. And given that my own folks were prone to dishing out hidings to me when I acted up, I would always run to my grandparents for protection. For some reason, my dad was allowed to discipline me (for discipline, read knock seven bells out of me) if I got out of hand, but when my mum tried to do it, my grandma would not allow it as she felt the responsibility had been handed to her. It was only when we moved out of my grandparents' home a few years later that my mum was even allowed to be my mum. So that was tough and weird.

Generally speaking, I was a bit of a nightmare. I just didn't give two hoots about anything. I was carefree and proud of it. So if I broke something, it wouldn't bother me. My dad would hit the roof and I think it was mainly because I showed no sign of remorse or sorrow for any damage I might do in my actions. This also extended to my relationship with Mako. While he was in New Zealand, I was the top dog who was running the show at my grandparents' place. Meanwhile, over the water, he was ruling the roost in his domain with no other kid to challenge his position as the mini gaffer. Suddenly, we were thrust together under one roof and all hell broke loose. I don't think either one of us could understand what was going on, so we fought all the time, refusing to accept each other. There was always friction between us. My parents had to work really hard to make us understand that we were brothers, but that's a really tough thing to do when you've been parted at the most crucial time in the development of your relationship. We got there in the end, of course, but I'm certain those early years will always affect our relationship.

I'm not saying all this because I'm looking for sympathy. I'm just saying what happened because it was a defining and important moment in my life, one that I barely remember, but something which clearly helps explain things in my childhood.

Like me sitting silently in a school interview for no reason.

Like me eating all the pies and sleeping for half a day.

Like so many other stories in subsequent years which I'll tell you soon enough.

My ancestry and those early years in Tonga shaped who I am. And returning there every summer continued to make an impression on me and show me the other side of the largely Western culture I was experiencing in Wales during the rest of the year. Sione remained a huge influence on me and our family, continuing to drive us forwards to make lives for ourselves in the UK.

For a policeman and taxi driver, his vision was extraordinary. He was a rugby player too and represented his country with distinction, going on to coach the Tongan national team to its most famous ever win, and arguably the greatest upset in international rugby history. In 1973, Sione took a team of virtual unknowns to Australia to play two Test matches. The first one went as expected with the Tongans going down to a heavy defeat in Sydney, but in Brisbane it was a different story as a spirited display saw us run in four tries to Australia's two and record an astonishing

16–11 win. It's hard to do justice to just how big a result this was for Tongan rugby.

Even though Sione was a proud man, he was always humble and it wasn't like he spent every day telling us about him masterminding the win over Australia. Instead, he'd tell us about it every other day. I'm kidding, of course. He worked so hard, and when he wasn't being a policeman, he would get into his taxi and sit in town for hours on end waiting for a customer. The town centre of our capital city Nuku'alofa is not exactly as you would imagine your own town or city centre. Instead of hustle and bustle, there's the odd tumbleweed blowing across the street if you're lucky. So he really would wait for hours. I can remember him returning home one day with a look of immense pride on his face as he told us that he picked up a fare and that the passenger had tipped him well so that he received more money than the journey was worth. Even today, I still remember that and tip any cab drivers that I use as I always remember Sione's face that day and the pride he had in telling us what had happened.

That was during one of those long summers back home. By then, I'd graduated from the 'pie and crash' regime at Ocean of Light and had joined my brother at the side school. I hated going to school there, but I knew there was nothing else to do every day, especially if my dad was there. There was no way he was going to tolerate us sitting around all day. Even when he had returned to the UK to start his pre-season training, he called my mum to check on us and he called Sione to make sure he was making us run, just like Sione used to make my dad and all his brothers run. But we were doing our running at school during epic games of stick rugby, which we'd play against the state school, who backed on to ours. We were separated by a rugby pitch and that's where battle would commence every lunchtime. The local kids would call me 'palangi' which translates to 'touching the sky'. Tongans think that white people were closer to the sky than us because they're taller than we are, so they call most white foreigners 'palangi'. Which meant I was a 'palangi' too, despite the fact that I was neither white nor foreign. But that didn't seem to matter.

● ● ●

I'm running with a stick in my hand, heading for the try line.

From nowhere, I'm suddenly bundled straight off the pitch and some kid is sitting on my chest.

Other kids are screaming. With joy.

I can hear, 'Get the palangi!' ringing in my ears.

I get up, dust myself down, while my adversary takes the stick on to the pitch to restart the game.

I line up back on the playing area next to Mako with a grin on my face.

The game restarts and my heart is thumping away.

I'm chasing everything that moves. If there was a cheetah on this pitch, I swear I'd hunt it down and catch it.

The kid that took me out is gonna get it back.

But he doesn't have the stick, so I'd better leave him for the time being.

The chicken nuggets are weighing heavy in my belly as I maraud across the pitch, chasing that stick. I may as well be a frigging dog.

But this is way better than break time in the UK. Just weeks ago, we were playing Bulldog there but there's not much in it for me. I just run through the other kids there as they're all small.

Here, these kids are more like me. They are big units who take pleasure in smashing each other and making sure nobody else is going to do better than them. My kind of people. Actually, my people.

'Get the palangi!' someone yells as I grab the stick off another kid and flatten him at the same time.

My kind of people.

I'm running as fast as I can now. And I'm going to score. Nobody is catching me now.

I run back and someone else calls out 'palangi' at me.

'I'm one of you guys,' I protest at nobody in particular. 'I can speak Tongan and everything.'

I even speak Tongan to my cousins while I'm there and we avoid English on purpose, the complete opposite of life in the UK. But nobody seems to particularly care.

'This is the English guy,' they might sometimes say if they're choosing a polite way to single me out as different.

On this rugby pitch at lunchtime though, I am definitely a palangi.

I shrug my shoulders and get on with the game.

I'm chasing everything again. God, I love this. Absolutely love it.

The sun is shining. I'm chasing a stick around on a rugby pitch. Life is good.

Suddenly, everyone is walking in different directions. Away from the pitch. What the hell has happened?

● ● ●

It's over. Lunchtime is over. I swear it goes quicker every day.

The state school boys are heading back in the direction of their school. We're walking back towards the side school.

Yet wherever we're going, we're all currently doing the same thing: dressing ourselves appropriately for the afternoon.

I try to button up my shirt which is wide open. But it's not happening.

I look down and realise I have buttons missing and a rip in the fabric large enough to put my hand through.

Oh crap.

If you're not dressed properly for school, you're going to get a beating. Those are the rules.

I'm going to have to be one of those boys who spends the whole afternoon sitting a certain way so that the teacher can't see that my shirt has been shredded.

This is going to be awkward.

As I get into my classroom, I tie the shirt up at the bottom so that it doesn't look open and slide into my chair carefully so as not to upset the delicate way I've made this thing look like it's functioning normally.

The teacher is in the room now and the lesson is underway. My arms and hands are sitting in front of my chest, and I'm positioned at a slight angle to the teacher – from her point of view, I am an exemplary pupil of the Tonga side school, dressed immaculately and ready to learn and absorb information and education like some kind of mad clever sponge.

From my point of view, I'm a sweaty nine-year-old who has just spent around forty minutes chasing a stick across 100 metres of a grassy field and is now sitting in a classroom in torn clothes, not paying any attention to what the teacher is saying, focusing only on making sure this person doesn't see the offending, damaged item.

There is at least one hour left of school now, but I can do this. I haven't moved position once for around forty-five minutes and everything is beginning to hurt. Everything inside me needs to shift around a bit, but I cannot risk moving now in case the full extent of the terrible state of my shirt is revealed.

There will be pain, but the pain of the branch on my buttocks will be worse so this pain is actually good.

My legs are cramping, but it's OK. This is good pain.

Time is not playing to the same rules that it played during the stick rugby game. It was on fast forward then, but now it's practically come to a standstill.

I've got pins and needles in my right leg. I desperately want to move it. But I can't give in. I cannot let it go at this late stage. We must be minutes away from the end of the day.

I feel like everybody is watching me, but when I turn my head it seems that not one person is looking in my direction. I suddenly realise that even that turn of the head was a dangerous manoeuvre and could've resulted in my capitulation and surrender.

I must stay focused.

And now I can hear the sound of heaven. The sound of victory. The sweet sound of freedom. It is, of course, the ringing of the school bell which signals the end of the day and means that I can finally move, and carefully extract myself from this highly dangerous situation.

I wait until the teacher is out of my eyeline, and very carefully slide out *of my seat, still holding everything together so that it all looks perfectly normal.*

I'm out of the classroom and out of danger.

Yes, I've done it. I win!

Now, I just have to show this shirt to my mum . . .

● ● ●

That's how it was until I was around eleven and stopped returning to Tonga so regularly. The scrapes, the sticks, the branches, the shirts – it was all very much a huge part of my life. Don't get me wrong, I am now an Englishman who takes the maximum amount of pleasure and pride from my red rose shirt every single time I pull it on. But I can't help where I'm from, so I will always have a massive connection with Tonga. It's part of who I am and always will be. That's why when Tonga beat Italy in 2016, the UK papers ran a story that Mako and I had paid for the drinks for the celebrating Tongan players. Which wasn't strictly true, but I guess we had indirectly helped them to mark the win in style.

My dad became the CEO of Tonga Rugby, and he does it for the love of the sport and his country. It's not something he really makes money out of. Seeing him do that, teaches me so much about what's important in life. He's giving something back. And that's exactly what I do with a lot of the money we earn from playing for Saracens and England.

We're lucky enough to be playing in a professional era where elite players can earn very decent money. We're not talking anywhere near Premier League football levels, but we can live well from our careers. But I don't sit on that money. A lot of it goes to my parents, and back to family in Tonga. We also have a lot of cousins at some of the best schools here, following in our footsteps – so that money goes to people who need it way more than I do.

So when my dad was putting his hand in his pocket to buy drinks for the team after that famous victory, it's likely that the source of that money might have been Mako and myself. We're on a WhatsApp group with a lot of Tongan lads, including one of the players that day, and he was telling us how my dad was getting the drinks in, and the rest of the team were egging him on, telling him to buy more, because Mako and I had just picked up bonuses from playing for England that same day. When my mum heard, her reaction was, 'I don't know how he's paying for drinks, because he's supposed to be working for free,' which made me realise he must have used some of our money.

Good for him and good for them.

Just as long as none of them call me palangi.

5

Breaking Bad

I've got the gun in my hand.

I'm completely calm, my hand's not shaking or anything.

I shift around on the uncomfortable wooden stool. These things are not meant to be sat on for longer than about ten minutes. But I've been sat here for way longer than that, bored out of my mind.

The gun is starting to weigh heavy in my hand.

I look down at it.

It feels so cool to be holding it. It's black, sleek and dangerous. Just how I like my guns.

I'm still feeling calm, more bored than ever, although this gun is definitely making things more interesting.

Right now, I reckon I'm probably the only kid in the country who's sitting in a science lesson while holding a gun.

The really strange thing is, it doesn't seem that abnormal to me.

● ● ●

Before the lesson started my mate Rich Carter told us he was selling his BB gun for a fiver. As luck would have it, I found a fiver in my pocket. I have no idea where this note came from. It must have been fate, but my heart barely skipped a beat as I handed it over to him, and took the gun in return.

● ● ●

I'm still holding it. The teacher is talking about science stuff and scribbling something on the whiteboard. I can't really hear her. I can only hear the gun. I can only hear it pleading with me to fire it.

I know how mad it would be for me to do that right here, right now, in the classroom. I know that makes no sense, but I also know that it would be insane and I want to know what will happen.

It's like a science experiment. Except a lot more interesting than the one the teacher is talking about at the moment.

She's drawing some equations on the whiteboard. They don't make much sense to me. I look down at the gun again. I move my finger to the trigger.

'Imagine firing it now straight into the floor,' I think to myself.

I'm tempted to pull the trigger, but I can't do it. Yet.

I look around at Rich Carter to show him the gun. But he's not looking at me. He's looking at the whiteboard.

I switch my attention back to the whiteboard and then back to the gun.

'OK,' I think. 'Let's do this.'

I hold the gun up in my right hand, I've got my finger back on the trigger.

I glance around and nobody can see me. Everybody is looking at the board. And I'm now staring hard at it too, as I pull the trigger not once, but twice.

BANG! BANG!

Somebody's screaming. And they're screaming loud.

My face has gone white.

It's the teacher screaming and it continues for a while.

She's livid.

The pellets hit the board hard, near her hand. But not on it.

I'm shocked.

The screaming has stopped.

Everyone in the class is looking confused and are turning their heads in three different directions all at once.

'Who the hell did that?' asks the teacher.

I think for less than a split second. I think about whether I can pretend I have nothing to do with this. It's less time than it takes to blink. And before I even realise it, my hand is up in the air, faster than a bullet out of a gun, and I say, 'It was me.'

'Come outside,' she says.

I'm finally off that horrible stool and I'm walking out of the classroom. I look at Rich Carter again but he's not making eye contact with me. Fair enough.

I'm still not entirely sure what the fuss is all about. OK, it was a silly thing to do, but she's not hurt and I could never have hurt her with that thing. Could I?

● ● ●

I had to see the Castle School headmistress and she told me how serious this was. I still couldn't understand why it was such a big problem. It wasn't like it was a real gun, firing real bullets or anything like that. But I was dumb. And I was naive. And I was also likely to be suspended from school for a few days, according to the headmistress. That didn't sound like bad news to me. Yes, my parents were going to kill me but apart from that, this might not turn out too bad.

School had finished by then and it was time for rugby training. That was definitely better than going home, because I knew my dad would have been waiting for me there and the longer I could put that off, the better. Rich Carter was training too, so I confided in him.

'I am so scared about going home,' I said.

'Me too,' he replied. 'My mum's gonna yell at me.'

'Yell at you?' I said. 'I wish my mum was only going to shout at me.' But he didn't understand about that. Nobody did.

● ● ●

My mum is armed with a broom and she's trying to jab the end of the handle at me. I'm cowering in front of her in our living room.

I know I have to take the punishment, but I can't help trying to resist.

She thrusts the broom towards me, but I instinctively raise my arm to block its impact.

'Stop blocking me!' she says firmly.

'I can't, it's natural!' I reply.

She jabs the handle in my leg. I can't block that one in time.

I have to take it. I can't fight back. It's not right.

And I can't show any weakness but my leg is hurting from the last hit.

'Do you know how embarrassing you are?' she says.

I look at her as if to say, 'Yes, I do know . . . I don't know why I do these things,' but it's not so easy to communicate that with my eyes.

'Everyone else is doing so well at school and you're the only one who gets letters home, detentions, and you're the only one who gets suspended!'

The handle comes down at me again, straight into my raised arm, clumping into a bit of flesh and bone. Ouch.

'Why am I always doing this to myself?' I think as I prepare to defend myself from another whack. It's about this time during a hiding that I always start to question myself. If this is always the outcome of my daft behaviour, then why do I keep doing stupid things?

BOOM! The side of the broom crashes into my leg again. That one stings a bit.

'Why the hell do I do this?' I think again as I look up, hoping that my mum has had enough.

I look at my arms and legs and they're covered in these red marks, roughly the shape of the end of the broom handle. It's not a good look. My mum looks at them too and walks out of the room.

We're done. It's over. For now.

● ● ●

We're back at school now. I'm there with my dad because the school have asked me to come in. He's taken time off work so he's already unhappy.

We're sitting with this really smug guy, Mr Smart and he's really enjoying being in control of this situation, telling us how it is.

'So we had a talk last night,' he's saying. 'All the heads of year talked, and we've decided that Billy is going to be suspended from school for two weeks.'

'Yes!' I think to myself.

'Fe'ao, just so you know the severity of the incident, I'm going to give you the gun to hold.'

Smart passes the BB gun to my dad and he holds it.

He holds it some more and then he looks at me and he's getting really angry now.

'It feels like a real gun, it could've killed someone,' says Smart, making matters even worse.

'But I didn't mean to kill anyone,' I protest.

'Yeah, I know, but you don't know what could've happened,' says Smart.

I now know how stupid I was. I worked it out the day before but it's only now, sitting here with my dad, that I can't believe what a fool I am.

My dad's still holding the gun. I don't think he's going to shoot me in front of Smart but he's still looking angry.

Suddenly, from nowhere, Dad is asking Smart what's being done about Rich Carter, the boy who brought the gun into school.

Come on, Dad! Get in there! He wants to know if he's also going to be disciplined in the same way.

Yes, Dad!

Smart's squirming. He's got no answers. This is cool.

Suddenly, we're walking out of the room and heading home – and I'm looking forward to a two-week bonus holiday.

● ● ●

If only. If only it was a holiday. If only I hadn't got home and taken another hiding – two punishments for the same crime – from my dad. I can laugh about it now, but at the time I was thinking, 'When is this gun thing going to actually run out, or am I going to be in trouble forever?'

Worse was to follow, as not only did my dad absolutely destroy me with a two-week training camp that I will never forget, I also had to do loads of homework every day to make up for all the school lessons that I was missing. That was one of the hardest fortnights ever. I had to run every day, and each time it felt like it was never going to end. And all the time I was thinking whether I was lucky to still be allowed back to the school after nearly shooting a teacher during a lesson.

The Castle School could've easily expelled me for that. Let's be honest, other kids may well have got the boot for it. But I'd just played for England

Under-18s at the age of fifteen and, without trying to sound big-headed, it was probably quite a good thing for the school to have me there.

I think that BB gun incident was kind of a turning point for me. I'm not suggesting that I didn't get into trouble at school again, because I definitely did, but I was getting pretty fed up with that whole cycle of doing daft stuff, getting a hiding, doing more daft stuff and getting another hiding. There had to be another way.

Having said all that, my dad did strike a blow for me against the school when he asked why it was only me taking all the heat for the crime. I'm not sure he had a point on this particular incident, because I had been so stupid to shoot that gun in the classroom. But, in more general terms, I think this might have been the moment when he understood that occasionally I was victimised. Whether that was because of my skin colour, or because I was always close to daft stuff going on is open to debate, but it's a fact that I was always getting into trouble.

Perhaps I should have been smarter and distanced myself from the action, but when I was younger, I never thought things through properly. I just acted impulsively, without ever engaging my brain.

Once, in another science lesson, we were dissecting a pig's eye. An interesting enough activity to keep most teenagers occupied and free from distraction, but not me. The teacher had left the room and there was a bit of tomfoolery when some of my classmates attempted to throw their Pritt Sticks up to the ceiling to see if they would stick up there. I saw that as an invitation to take it one step further, because that's what I'm like. I grabbed a pig's eye, and said, 'Try this!' and launched it up to the ceiling. Sure enough, it stuck there like glue.

That brief moment of pride and joy at having done something cool like that was suddenly replaced by the fear of what I had actually just done – otherwise known as the moment when my brain kicked into gear.

'Please come down, please come down,' I pleaded to it using the power of my thoughts. With one eye on the classroom door and one on the eye in the sky, I was desperately hoping it would drop down in the nick of time. But it wasn't to be.

Seconds later, the door opened, the teacher walked in, took one look at the ceiling which was where everyone's eyes were fixed, then turned to me and said, 'Billy, was that you?' Busted.

The people who grew up around me like Josh Faletau and Anthony Maka always tell me how tough I had it as a kid. It's true that I always used to take the heat but that's because I was the loud one, the one who would put myself out there in people's faces. I was always the naughtiest kid, the one to chat back to my parents, the one who had something right to say even though it's wrong, just to challenge them. An annoying little so-and-so, essentially. I was not as smart as my brother Mako, I would just act on emotion. If I felt like doing something, I would just go ahead and do it and deal with the consequences later.

Consider the time my family and I were all watching the Champions League final between Manchester United and Chelsea in 2008. We were all supporting Man United because they wear red and our school in Tonga wore red – that was the only reason. My dad decided to support Chelsea just to be against us. So John Terry missed his penalty, and we all celebrated because Man United went on to win. When Sir Bobby Charlton led the Man United team to get their medals and the trophy, my dad told us

'Bobby Charlton is United's ambassador' and me being me, for no particular reason other than my dad had backed Chelsea, replied to him, 'What do you know about him? He's from Man United!'

'Oi!' yelled my dad. 'Shut up and go and do some work!'

By that stage, everyone had left the room, leaving me in peace to wind my dad up until he flipped. So I took his cue and drifted out of the room, heading to the kitchen where everyone else had gathered. As I arrived at the doorway, still in sight and sound of the TV room, I pointed my fingers as if I was shooting a gun, pulled the fake trigger, and promptly broke wind, to the delight and amusement of everyone in the kitchen. As they all laughed, my dad called out, 'Billy, was that you, did you fart?' to which I replied, 'Yes!' with a smile on my face. But that was just the excuse he was looking for, and he dished out a hiding to me for my impertinence. Harsh? Maybe. But, that was me to a tee – everyone knew where the line was but I would always just carry on and take it too far.

The thing is, I believe that whatever was dished out to me by my parents was fully deserved. I only got smacked if I was doing something wrong. You don't shoot a teacher with a BB gun, get home and have your parents say to you, 'Right, go to your room.' What would you learn from that? I know that if I'd have been left to my own devices, I'd be struggling. They also taught me important lessons about how you treat people.

The thing that always stuck in my head was my dad saying, 'Treat the teacher like you want your mum to be treated, and treat your girlfriend like you'd want your sisters to be treated.' As I got older I wasn't necessarily wiser, but I was less likely to swear at a teacher and I always tried to apologise if I did anything stupid. It's funny, because when you're kind to people, they're usually kind back to you, but I didn't realise that as a twelve-year-old. You just want to be rebellious all the time.

After I got a hiding, I'd run up to my room and shout into my pillows, 'Why did my dad marry this wicked lady?' I remember really not liking my mum because I was a petulant and stupid kid. But I love my mum so much now, because I can see what my behaviour was like and how hard it must have been for her.

Eventually, they gave up on dishing out hidings to me. I remember my mum saying, 'I don't even want to smack you anymore. We don't think it's working, so we're going to talk to you about why it's wrong.' And when they did talk to me, I felt that was way more effective than them smacking me, but maybe I was a bit more mature at the time.

She probably said that soon after I'd returned to school following the BB gun incident, because it wasn't long before I did something stupid again. This time, instead of shooting a teacher, I chucked an egg at one. I just couldn't help myself when the opportunity arose. The teacher in question was a particularly annoying science tutor who was watching over all the kids one lunchtime. A gang of us were hiding in a bush, having procured some eggs from the teacher's science room. And when I say procured, I mean we nicked them.

Our target was sitting about twenty metres from us, sipping his lunchtime cup of tea, surveying the scene before him, except us. One of the guys with me, threw an egg in the teacher's direction and missed by a mile. An obvious ploy to try to lure someone else into thinking they could do a better job, but one which I fell for hook, line and sinker. 'Gimme one of them!' I said instantly, grabbing an egg and hurling it straight at the teacher. Direct hit. It landed, and smashed into bits, on the shoulder of his jacket. He spun around to see me still standing in my throwing position with a puzzled look on my face – a look which said, 'Why the hell did I just do that?' But I knew why I did it. I did it because I saw everything as a competition and just wanted to be the best. Useful on the rugby pitch, but not so useful in an egg-throwing-at-teacher game of dare.

Another impulsive act was going to cost me big as I was suspended again, this time for two days. But this was the moment where my parents almost gave up on me and didn't bother giving me a thrashing. And it was way more effective because, for the first time the hurt I was causing my parents began to sink in, and I started to think about things just a tiny bit more. That breakthrough was years in the making, because I'd been doing daft stuff for such a long time.

● ● ●

I'm staring through the window at the bike and I really want to ride it. But I can't ride it because I'm not feeling well.

I'm the only kid in the Faletaus' house, home alone with my mum and Josh and Toby's mum. The boys are all in school. I'm bored. It's no fun without them. I don't feel great, but being bored makes me feel even worse.

I don't even know what's wrong with me, but my mum said I couldn't go to school so here I am, stuck at home.

I'm still staring out of the window. The sky is a light grey. It might rain, it might not. It probably will rain though, because it rains a lot here. I like this place, but it's not like home. It's not like Longo Longo where the sun shines every day and I'm not poorly like I am today so I can go to school with all my cousins.

The grey sky behind the brightly coloured bike makes it stand out. I want to ride it. I have to ride it. Mako, Josh and Toby have all ridden it before. I've watched them ride that bike down the hill by the Ebbw Vale clubhouse so many times, but I've never been on it. It's not fair. Riding down that hill looks like so much fun.

I think I feel better. I think I feel well enough to ride that bike. I am definitely well enough to ride that bike down that hill. But how can I with my mum, and Josh and Toby's mum at home with me?

That bike wants me to ride it though, I can tell. It definitely wants to fly down that hill with me on board. It's practically asking me to do it. So if I was to sneak out of here right now, it wouldn't really be my fault. The bike is making me.

I can hear the women nattering, chattering with the sound of the TV in the background. They can't hear me. If I can hear them and they can't hear me then I have an advantage. I can disappear for a few minutes. I can ride that bike down that hill, drag it back up again and I'll be back before they even realise that I've gone.

I'm leaving the house right now. I'm creeping out of the back door. My heart is beating faster than usual.

Now, I have the bike's handlebars in my hands and I'm clambering aboard the little beauty. Finally, I'm sitting on the bike and it feels good.

I walk with the bike halfway down the hill and then I begin to pedal, but it's harder work than it should be. Eventually, I start rolling down the hill.

The bike is feeling a bit rickety.

I look down and see that one of the tyres is flatter than the average pancake. Why didn't I notice this before I got on? I try to find the brakes with my hands, but I can't feel anything under the handlebars.

I look down. There are no brakes. No brakes and a flat tyre.

Why didn't I notice this before I got on?

I can't think why but it doesn't matter anyway as I'm picking up speed and momentum now and there's not much I can do.

I'm flying down the hill on this bike and this is exactly what I wanted to do. I'm not looking out of the window miserably, I'm actually doing what feels good.

But it's also scary because I can't stop.

In front of me, several Ebbw Vale rugby players are walking across the bottom of the hill, heading to morning training.

Oh crap.

I swerve around one, who looks startled.

I swerve around another.

I can't stop.

Oh crap.

There's a river at the bottom of the hill.

And I can't stop.

In a second, I will be in the river unless I jump off the bike now.

But if I jump off the bike now, I will really hurt myself. The water will make for a better landing.

I can't stop anyway.

I hit the water. I'm off the bike, in the river and, at last, I have stopped.

It's not deep, but it's cold and a bit of a shock to suddenly be submerged in a river when I just wanted to take the bike for a quick ride down the hill.

I'm crying. I'm properly bawling my eyes out as one of the players, Jason Strange, wades in to help me. He drags me out of the water, and now we're marching back up the hill towards the house.

I'm feeling shocked and nervous.

Shocked because I just rode a bike straight into a river, nervous because I now have to face my mum, who currently thinks I'm ill in bed. This is not going to go well.

Jason and I have reached the house, I'm not exactly pegging it towards the door, but he half has his arm around my shoulder in support and is half pushing me along as the condemned man, or boy, that I am.

Jason's knocking on the door now.

I'm looking down. There is no way I'm going to look up and see those faces of rage.

I can hear the door open.

I look up. Oops, didn't mean to do that.

My mum's jaw drops. Josh's mum is wide-eyed.

I look down again.

Jason's telling them what happened. He's saying words like 'bike', 'river', 'help' and 'tears' – my mum's saying words like 'bed' and 'ill' but I'm not really listening.

Into the house I go. Mum doesn't quite pull me in by the ears but it's not the friendliest welcome home I've ever received.

And the hiding that's going to follow won't be either.

● ● ●

By the time the others came home from school I'd recovered from the beating, but was still feeling down in the dumps. And poorly. Really.

'What the hell were you doing?' said Mako.

I had no idea what the hell I was doing so I couldn't really explain why I'd ridden a bike with no brakes and a flat tyre down a hill and into a river.

Mako and Toby were laughing, and Josh was doing his best not to laugh, but was basically laughing too. Then they discovered that the bike was still in the river and they were less impressed.

'You should've brought the bike back with you,' said Toby.

'No way! No!' said my mum.

'None of you are ever riding that bike!' added Josh and Toby's mum.

Mako, Toby and Josh looked at me with far less pity and a great deal more contempt.

'Mate, you're a friggin' idiot,' said Mako. 'Not only have you ruined it for yourself, you've now ruined it for us as well,' he added as it sunk in that none of them would be flying down the hill on that bike again.

I felt bad. But not too bad. If I was going down, I always knew it was better if others were going down with me.

Doing daft stuff like riding a bike into a river came naturally to me. My childhood was littered with incidents which would all lead to the familiar denouement of a hiding and a resolution not to behave like that again, only for me to repeat the whole process as soon as I had half a chance.

The hidings always followed the same pattern. My mum or dad would invite me into the living room to be disciplined. It wasn't the sort of invitation that you could turn down because you happened to have something else already planned for that particular moment. As a child, I had to put my bravest face on and go and face the music in the living room. The music might take the shape of my dad's belt or my mum's broom handle. It would be so hard not to cry at the punishment and the pain, and sometimes I would even have a cry before being disciplined, but that would lead to laughter and teasing from my siblings because the culture dictates that's not what you do – you have to front up to it and deal with the consequences of what you've brought on yourself. Because it's not like I'd be disciplined for no good reason. In fact, there would always be a very good reason, whether it was misbehaving at school, getting in trouble with the referee on the rugby pitch or back-chatting to my parents.

The worst day of the year for me was always Parents Evening at school. I always looked at that as a chance for the teachers to get their own back on me. They'd tell my mum things like 'he's so disruptive' because I was. They were never harsh, just truthful. I figured it was worth one or two bad days a year – if Parents Evening was every Friday I would have acted like an angel at school, because otherwise I would have been rumbled by the teachers every week. But, once or twice a year was fine and I could handle that. Even then, I would still be on my best behaviour throughout the evening, carrying my mum's bags, and walking a few steps behind her out of respect. Despite everything I did to stay on her good side, it never helped because the minute we returned home, the invitation to the living room would be issued for me.

It was all deserved, as I've said, but I also think my parents were trying to make sure I didn't stray too far from the family, to keep me in line as much as possible. My dad's oldest brother was also raised by his grandparents for a time – or adopted as we call it in Tonga – and while it was way longer than the time I had spent with my grandparents, my parents were keen to make sure that I didn't feel like a stranger to our family, as my uncle had after he moved back with his parents. My dad felt that his brother would just come to their house to eat and get changed and was more like a visitor than a member of the family, so he wanted to do everything in his power to make sure that would never happen with me. Hence, the strict discipline and trying to keep me in line so that I would behave more like Mako and my sisters and be a part of the family.

Whatever the theory, and whatever the outcomes, I was the kid who I was and that meant I was spontaneous and carefree throughout my childhood. Sometimes, though, a little too carefree.

● ● ●

The ball's there and I'm having it. I'm not done yet.

A ruck forms and I'm all over it. I'm all over it and now I have it and I'm going to run with it again. Here we go, I'm on my way.

Oh no, what's the referee blowing his whistle for? That can't be for anything I've done, can it? I was about to go and score again, I'm so annoyed.

I'm the captain so I can approach the referee to find out what's going on.

He tells me that I went off my feet and dived over the ruck to get the ball.

'I didn't,' I say. I know I'm not supposed to argue, but I'm not having this bloke tell me I did something wrong when I didn't.

'You did,' he says.

I'm about to lose it, this is completely unfair.

'That's bullcrap,' I say and march off before he can send me off.

I look over to the sports pitch next to ours and the girls are playing hockey. Maybe they can see me. Maybe they can see me standing up for what's right. That'll impress them.

I carry on walking to the side of the pitch where Lloyd Spacey is waiting for me, looking a lot less impressed than he was when I was scoring tries and kicking conversions earlier in the game.

But I don't care.

I don't care about him or any of this.

'Calm down, Billy,' he says.

'No, I'm going home,' I say. Because that's what I really want to do, I want to carry on walking straight off this pitch and just go back to my house, up the road from the school.

'Right, if you go home, we'll deal with all this in the morning,' he says, and I'm already on my way before he's even finished speaking.

I glance over at the hockey girls. They will love this. I'm the rebel without a cause. I'm not sure if any of them can see me though.

It doesn't take me long to walk home. It takes me slightly longer than it should though, because I still have my boots on and they're a bit annoying to walk in. But I don't really care. I just want to get home and forget about that stupid game.

I get home, still in my kit and boots but my parents aren't around yet. I tell Mako what happened. He doesn't say much. He never does.

● ● ●

It's the morning now. The morning which Space was referring to when he said we'll deal with it. I'm by my locker at school, and Mako rushes over to me to tell me I need to write a letter of apology to Spacey. He's been to see him to find out what's going on and to see if he's going to tell my mum and dad. I need to write this letter. Thanks, Mako!

I grab some paper and a pen and, suddenly full of remorse, guilt and fear, I write. I write like I've never written before. The words flow from my pen like a William Shakespeare play.

'Dear Mr Spacey,' I write. 'Apologies for my behaviour which was unacceptable.'

That's a good start, that's a really good start. So strong and meaningful.

What else do I write? Come on, think!

'Please can I still be captain of the Year 7 rugby team?' I add.

That'll do. That's brilliant, that is. It's poetry.

I dash round to Spacey's office and hand him the note I've just written.

He reads it, smiles and thanks me.

'Are you going to tell my parents?' I ask him.

'Yes, I have to tell them,' he says.

Oh crap.

● ● ●

You can imagine what happened next. But just because I was disciplined by my parents regularly does not mean I did not have a happy and wholesome upbringing. Being raised with a loving, close-knit family and my boys Toby, Josh and Anthony Maka, meant that I was lucky. Our gang spent so much time together growing up that it was like being raised in a summer camp or something. We hung out together all the time, laughing, joking, playing and running. There was so much running, with my dad barking out the orders, but that's another story.

Almost from the moment we set foot in the UK, we were in the company of the gang, or several members of the gang at least. During the 1999 World Cup, we all moved into the Faletaus – that was when I decided to ride that bike into the river behind their house. From then on, we were pretty much inseparable. The only time we couldn't all be together was when we went to school down the road from their house, the reason being that I was too young to be in the same playground as the others. Even though I was the same size as them, I was in the junior part of the school and we had our breaks in a separate playground. I remember being able to see their play area from ours but only being allowed to look longingly at them, desperate to be reunited.

Even when we moved to Bristol, Josh and Toby would still visit. And they actually moved in with us a few years later because they both went to school at Filton College in Bristol. That was probably the best time of my life and we still talk about it to this very day.

We'd all sleep in our converted garage. It was absolutely freezing beyond belief in the winter, but we were there together so somehow it didn't really matter. We'd go to sleep with our jackets on and wrap ourselves up in sleeping bags. In the morning, we'd wake up and it would be so cold in there, that we'd immediately see the breath coming out of our mouths. My nose was like ice, my hands were like freezer blocks, but it didn't matter because it was just so awesome to be with the boys. They were like family – and not just the ones who were actually family. Being around the boys made me feel like I was back in Tonga, but there we were in Bristol living completely different lives.

We all had the same strict parents who didn't want us getting into any trouble. They were very concerned about impressionable kids like us getting into drink and made sure we knew the dangers. They drilled that into us so much that for us, the equivalent of a mad night out was a trip to Tesco to buy the groceries for my mum. We'd stroll through the town wearing vests, shorts and flip flops, and tossing a rugby ball between ourselves, as if we were cruising around Longo Longo, except there we were in Thornbury where it wasn't particularly warm and there wasn't any white sand within about 100 miles of the place. But that didn't bother us. And neither did the lack of drink, even if both were plentiful in Tesco – we were together, laughing, joking, poking fun, hanging out, and that was good enough.

If we weren't picking up milk, fruit and veg, another weekly night out for us was the short trek across the field to visit my mum's church on a

Sunday night. But not for prayer, we'd done that in the morning. This was the regular clean-up operation which we took great delight in executing, mainly because it was more time alone where we could all be free. Yes, cleaning up a church is a different kind of freedom but that doesn't mean it was ever taken for granted.

Bonding like that at a young age set us up for life. Even though Mako, Toby and myself have gone on to have international rugby careers and developed close ties with a whole load of new guys we play alongside regularly, there is nothing to compare with those days and that crew. Josh is now married and living in Australia but that doesn't change anything. That closeness between our gang endures wherever we are in the world.

But none of them could've helped me on the day I got banged by Marcus Taylor – Marcus, this is your fifteen minutes, enjoy it! I loved the Castle School, but it was so loose that we could almost get away with anything, other than shooting teachers.

One day, we were at the bottom of the school field having a boxing fight. Some lad had brought in some boxing gloves and a few of us were trying them on for size and then also trying to put them to use. Now, this is not me making excuses but I have an extremely bloody nose. That means it doesn't take much for it to gush out blood all over the place, whether it's in a game or just messing around with mates. That day, Marcus, who was in my brother's school year, and I had the gloves on and we were exchanging punches. I threw a punch at Marcus and didn't connect that well and he simultaneously swung a glove at me and landed a slap perfectly on my nose. Instantly, my shirt was covered in the blood which was pouring from my nose. There was no time for retribution and we returned to our lessons. As I was walking to class, Space saw me and my now claret-spattered school shirt.

'What the hell happened?' he asked, somewhat startled by the state of me.

'Oh, we were fighting down the bottom of the field,' I replied.

He shook his head and carried on his way. It was that kind of school. I'm told that Marcus still dines out on being the only person to have banged me like that and got away with it so fair play to him, he's right. It was a bit of fun, and I would have been a hypocrite to get angry over it. But, if you're reading this Marcus, I'm ready for a rematch whenever you are!

The truth is it wouldn't have been the only conflict I got myself into during school. Everyone knew who I was very quickly as I kind of stood out, and other kids would never be afraid to throw dirt my way. Kids are always quick to point out differences whether it's size, colour or whatever. In the classroom, I was always fairly confident, but I could never be bothered. I knew that teachers became frustrated with me, because they could tell I had the ability but not the gumption to do anything with it. That changed as I matured, but I guess that initially I was just like loads of other teenagers in that I was a tad lazy. I was also someone who needed the right teacher to respond to – someone like Space just got me, and knew how I worked. Yes, we had all the rugby stuff to bond over, but he also understood where I was coming from in life. He was fantastic to all my family, not just Mako but also my sisters Tiffany and Ana, and he got on really well with my parents. He was similar to Jesse Coulson at Harrow School where I went after we left Bristol.

These characters were so important in guiding me on the right road when I could so easily have veered off course at any point. They were also essential members of my gang growing up, although not in the same way as my Tongan boys.

Back in Pontypool, Dawson 'Uncle Daws' Jones and Terry 'Tiger' Gordon also played hugely significant roles in my life, helping to make me and my family feel so welcome and at home in our new surroundings. Daws was, and still is, the man. When I was a kid, he was the coach of the Pontypool Schools team but he went above and beyond the call of duty with the way he looked after us.

He brought me rugby boots to play in, took me to training, organised pick-ups, drop-offs, the works, all so that my mum and dad didn't have to lift a finger. They were always so busy on the weekends, but Daws made sure that would never be a problem. He became part of the family, so I got to know him very well over my first three years in the UK. Daws would often pop into our house for a cup of tea, and a quick bite to eat. We understood each other very well when I was a kid and, even now, we still talk all the time. When I left Wales to move across the bridge to Bristol I wrote him a leaving letter, thanking him for all his help while I was playing for Pontypool Schools and also making him a solemn promise. 'I promise, Uncle Daws,' I wrote, 'that I'm never playing for England.' Unfortunately for Daws and all my Welsh mates, that was a promise I had to break. I think if you look at many things people say when they are kids, you'd be able to find some absolute belters to use against them in later life. When I moved to Bristol I could never have imagined that I'd be playing for England one day. Australia maybe, but England no way. But things change. They certainly did for me.

Playing for England now, it's funny how everyone talks about the 2003 World Cup winning team because my experience of that was so different. I was on the losing team that day! Growing up in Wales, everyone used to hate England. They were the enemy. On the day of that World Cup final, I definitely wanted Australia to win. Not only was my uncle playing for Brumbies in Canberra and my aunties living out there, I was also born in Sydney so it wasn't a very hard decision for me.

When England won that unforgettable game, I was so angry. 'I hate that Wilkinson guy,' I said to anyone within earshot. It took me about a decade to realise that Jonny Wilkinson is probably the hardest-working sportsman in the world. His dedication and commitment to rugby is unbelievable. Even now, he'll come into the England camp to practise his kicking by himself. He could just be chilling at home. It's not like he's about to play a game anytime soon, but there he is working hard. When I'm done, I'll be done. There will be none of that for me. But he's the man, and he went from me thinking he was a villain after the 2003 final to becoming one of my heroes.

My other all-time rugby hero has always been Jonah Lomu. I wasn't that into actually watching rugby when I was a kid, only playing it, but you couldn't keep your eyes off Lomu. I didn't get the nuances of rugby then, but I could look at this guy and see a six-foot-five giant of a man with an absolutely ripped body, who's faster than anyone on the pitch and I'd think, 'How the hell does he do it?' You can't watch someone like that and not be inspired.

Did I think Lomu would inspire me to play for England? No way. But, like I said, things change. Despite my broken promise, I think Uncle Daws forgave me. After England beat Scotland to win the Six Nations in 2016, he sent me a text message to say congratulations. I replied by sending him one back saying that I must always get lucky when playing for coaches called Jones. I think he must have liked that as I read about it in the papers a couple of days later.

On a par with Daws was Tiger, Pontypool's kit man who helped my dad so much when he first arrived in Wales in 1998. Tiger and his wife Jane are some of the loveliest and most decent people you will ever meet, and they essentially became our UK grandparents while we lived in Wales.

My dad's first port of call was Cwmbran where he lived in a small flat which was basic. And when I say basic, I mean it had no heating. My dad slept in his clothes with his coat on because it was so frigging cold in this place. Can you even imagine that? Tiger was an absolute star because he recognised how much my dad was struggling – here was a random Tongan who had come to visit the land of Captain Cook and Winston Churchill, the heroes he had learned about in school, landing with a massive bump at the reality of life in the country he had eulogised as a kid. But this rather rude awakening was softened by the generosity, kindness and love of the amazing community around him, not least from Tiger and Jane.

Tiger would visit my dad, who barely had a morsel to eat, let alone heating, and take him Wagon Wheels and Jaffa Cakes for sustenance. Not necessarily giants of the nutritional game, but certainly better than nothing at all. And before long, I would also be the recipient of such benevolence.

Once we joined my dad in Wales, we became regulars at Tiger and Jane's house.

As the kit man's wife, Jane would always prepare matchday essentials like Jaffa Cakes, biscuits and other sweet stuff that my dad and his team-mates would scoff for an extra pre-game boost in an age before energy bars and isotonic drinks. So when my dad, Mako and I would go over to the house before a game, Jane would whisk us into the lounge while my dad and Tiger talked in the other room. Once we were in there, she would put her finger to her lips before feeding us chocolate digestives with tea and we'd just sit there, munching away on the fuel that was supposed to get my dad and the guys through the game.

After a few minutes, my dad's voice would bellow, 'Where are the kids?'

'Don't worry,' replied Jane. 'You just keep talking to Tiger!'

Before we left the house, Jane would try to sneak a Jaffa Cake into my pocket. Once, my dad saw.

'Jane! That's for the team.'

'Don't worry,' she replied. 'I'll buy some more.'

I thought she was awesome. Especially when I had a Jaffa Cake in my pocket and she had just denied my undeniable father. My dad hated it when anyone would do something for us that meant they would go to any extra effort. He did not want people to go out of their way for any of his kids. As he saw it, behaviour like that would be detrimental to our development as humans.

'Jane, please don't do that for them, otherwise they will become spoilt,' he'd say about her various kindnesses.

As we saw it, behaviour like that was crucial to our development as humans who consume essential sugary treats.

But whether he liked it or not, my dad, and my mum, were indebted to Tiger and Jane for helping them out when they were too busy to see to us. Jane would often pick us up from school which was always a welcome sight for me and Mako as that meant we'd go to her place and have untold amounts of tea and biscuits. It also meant that we'd sit in front of the telly with Tiger and watch as much wrestling as was possible in the time we had until dad would pick us up. Tiger was a huge wrestling fan so we didn't even have to ask him to put it on for us, because he would have already been watching it. And when my dad finally arrived, Tiger would always convince him to let us hang out for a bit longer – 'Come on, Fe'ao, let the boys stay!' – so we could watch a few more minutes of the action with him. With a supporting cast like that and growing up with my little gang, I always felt like I was part of something. It's a feeling that remains to this day.

6

On the Run

I'm strolling through the field near our house in Thornbury and I'm happy.

I'm happy because I'm with Mako.

I'm happy because I'm with our cousin Anthony Maka.

I'm happy because the three of us are on our way to clean mum's church. It's our time to be free, to be together, to be alone and to have fun.

I know every inch of this field so well, as this is where Dad makes us run. It feels good to not be running in this field. Man, I hate running. I hate it so much.

But this is not training time. This is our time.

In a neighbouring field up ahead, I can see a large group of lads. They're making a lot of noise and, like us, look like they're having a good time.

Maybe when I'm older, I'll have that sort of a good time but right now at the age of twelve, a good time is cleaning the church by ourselves. That's all we need.

The group of lads are getting louder and larger as we draw nearer to them.

Our own chatter stops as we look over to them. There are around a dozen of them, mainly guys, but a couple of girls too.

They're holding beer cans, which they constantly swig from, gulping down the contents like thirsty camels.

What's that?

Someone's yelling at us.

One of them is screaming at us.

'What are you doing in our country?' shouts one of the really tall ones. He must be about eighteen or nineteen.

And that might also be how many beers he's had.

'F--- off!' screams another.

I'm gobsmacked.

I'm shaking.

I'm scared.

Mako and Maka don't say a word back.

I'm frozen to the spot, but I've heard this stuff before. Occasionally, we get this kind of thing from people who are frustrated with life for whatever reason, but Mum and Dad have always taught us never to answer back, just brush it off and carry on.

I'm thinking about that and, just as we start walking away, a half-full can of Foster's flies straight towards the three of us. It misses our heads by inches.

'Go back to your own country,' comes another voice, full of rage and hate.

Suddenly, Maka turns around and starts walking towards this large group. His face is dark. He's livid.

I'm so scared.

'Let's go guys,' I say. 'Let's just go to the church and clean it. Please.'

'Nah,' says Mako, who is also now walking towards the hooligans.

I'm absolutely trembling with fear.

'We have to stand up for ourselves,' says Maka.

'No, we don't,' I'm thinking. 'Not against ten blokes, we don't. Let's pick and choose very carefully the exact moments when we stand up for ourselves.' But I don't say any of this because I'm too busy being scared.

This is madness.

I'm desperate to get out of here.

'Mum and Dad have told us to always walk away,' I plead with them, as I find myself walking behind them, forming a little triangle, as we all head towards our enemies.

'Yeah,' says my brother. 'But they're not here.'

Oh crap. They mean business and I'm really not up for this. My bro and cousin are like fifteen and sixteen years old, I'm just a kid. A big kid, admittedly, but still a kid.

I don't want to fight anyone or anything.

I can feel my heart-rate rising and the adrenaline kicking in, but not in a good way.

If anything, I'm actually shaking at the prospect of what might happen.

Reluctantly, I lag behind the other two as they march into the next field. I can't see their faces but I bet they're full of anger and defiance while mine is just etched with worry.

As we get closer, the group seems to grow in numbers and each of them are getting bigger in size too. At least in my eyes, anyway. There are probably about a dozen big lads and three girls. The blokes seem drunk, their eyes are vacant and they continue to tip the cans down their throats.

'Boys, please just go, you're gonna get your heads kicked in!' says one of the girls. And the way she says it, I can tell she really means it. I can hear the fear and concern in her voice. She might also be a bit worse for wear herself, but this is a clear intervention meant to help us.

'No, we won't,' says Maka.

'Yes we will,' I plead. 'Can we please just go?' All I want to do is get out of there and go to the church, clean it, then get home. I definitely don't want to see how this whole scene plays out. Not if I have to actually be in it.

But it doesn't matter what I think. Because Mako and Maka are striding forward and I have no choice but to stay by their sides, or a little bit further back than them, and fight like a man. Like a twelve-year-old man.

Oh crap.

We're almost there now and one of the lads steps forward and walks towards us. 'All right then, we're starting, are we?' he kind of half-asks and half-tells us.

Before we've had time to consider his statement, we are quickly surrounded by five of this crew. Mako and Maka are still the two points at the top of our triangle, with me safely tucked in at the back.

'Oh my gosh,' is all I can think as my throat goes dry with fear.

There is no way back from here.

From here, nobody just walks away and loses face.

From here, somebody or everybody gets their heads kicked in.

Oh my gosh.

'We warned you,' says the same girl as before. 'You're gonna get your heads kicked in now,' she informs us, merely confirming what I'm thinking.

But now is not the time for thinking. My thinking is done. Now it's time for action, which we can all think about later.

As the lads put their beer cans down – they wouldn't want to waste any – one of them jumps high in the air and lands a kick right on Maka's face. Just like that. Without even saying please.

I'm startled.

Luckily, Maka is not.

He wears the kick like an MMA fighter and responds by landing several blows to the body and head of his attacker.

For the first time, the fear turns to excitement. There's hardly any time for feelings but I think I might even be starting to enjoy this, especially when I see my brother fly into a group of lads as if he was clearing out a ruck. He bowls two of them straight out while Maka now has his guy on the ground and he's about to thump him when the kid yells, 'Hey! No fighting on the floor!'

'But you just kicked him in the face!' I think to myself before I decide to enter the fray.

Another guy has put his can down and is breaking off a rather ominous-looking tree branch to attack us with. He can't see me coming so I fly at him from the side. If Mako can clear out a ruck, I can definitely steam into an authentic rugby tackle.

BOOM!

I clatter into this kid's ribs and knock the wind straight out of him. I land on top of him and he's struggling to breathe. He won't be hitting anyone with that branch for the time being.

Back on the main stage, Mako and Maka are filling in about three blokes each. It's an extraordinary sight and I can't help myself as I shout 'Yeeeeaaaaaaahhhh! Go on lads!'

If I only have to make the odd rugby tackle here and there, this might not be too bad after all.

And so it goes on, Mako and Maka doing all the work while I intervene occasionally in my specialist role as a steamroller, flattening out any problem areas.

I see one of the girls, you know the caring types who were trying to warn us away so that we wouldn't get a hiding, about to aim a kick at Mako's head – he's still on the ground, doing some of his finest work. As the girl takes aim, one of the other lads stops her so he can do it.

I sprint over to him as he's about to wind up and release and he takes one look at me running towards him and flees the scene.

And he's not the only one.

Soon, most of the group have backed off, each of them a little sore, a bit battered and blue after meeting the fury of Mako and Maka for the first time.

This looks to me a lot like a victory. We stood up for ourselves against these lads and it seems to have done the job. There's nobody left to fight, so the three of us start walking back out of the field.

But suddenly, one of the guys is back, getting right on our cases. He's probably a bit drunker than everyone else. Which might explain why he yells, 'Is that all you've got?'

Is he joking? It seems not.

'Mate,' I say. 'All your friends have given up. Go away!'

But this tall and skinny, hammered kid is persistent.

Not only is he persistent but I notice that he's also carrying a brick in his hand and is getting closer and closer.

A brick? Seriously?

The bloke is obviously off his head.

And before I've had time to even finish that thought, he launches the brick straight at us.

We dodge it. It wasn't a great throw as the guy's drunk.

But I'm really wound up now. The fight's over, we won – you don't go throwing bricks at us afterwards.

I pick it up and turn towards this idiot.

'Come on then! Throw it!' he says.

I have my arm swung back, ready to release and all sorts of things are going through my mind. The bloke is standing so close to me that I could really melt him with it if I let go.

But I could also get into trouble for this.

What if I seriously injure him?

As this stand-off continues, one of the girls is yelling to brick man. 'Come back! Come back! He's got a broken rib and he's got a black eye, come back now!'

But he doesn't listen to them. He's still inviting me to cave his head in with the brick for some reason.

Maka then interrupts. 'Billy, don't do it. You'll probably kill him because he's so high. He's off his head.'

What would my mum and dad say? What are they going to say about us fighting anyway? Nothing hopefully, as they won't know.

'Throw it!' he pleads again.

'Mate, you don't need to ask me. I'll throw it if I want to throw it.'

And as I say that, my rage lessens. I realise how pointless it would be to throw the brick.

So I drop it and we head off back through the other field and on to the church which is where I had always wanted to go before all this madness started.

Mako and Maka dust themselves down as we make our way towards the church.

We don't say much. There isn't that much to say right now.

We know what we've done. We know it's wrong because our parents always asked us not to, but we also know it's right because we stood up for ourselves.

We make it to the church without having to take out any more Thornbury locals and begin the work of cleaning and tidying everything from that morning's service.

Other than the sounds of books being piled on top of each other, and the floor being swept, it's quiet – until, suddenly, breaking the silence is the unmistakable wailing of a siren.

A police car.

It's the siren of a police car.

Oh crap.

We look at each other.

Still we don't say one word.

The siren is still wailing.

Those scumbags have called the cops on us. I can't believe it. The nerve. The absolute nerve.

We're all staring at each other now, listening to the siren.

Something's different though.

The noise is definitely getting fainter.

We still don't move or speak.

Wherever that police car is, it's not heading our way.

●　●　●

Our brush with the law was over.

Not that there ever was one. But when you're twelve years old and have just participated in your first major scrap, you cannot imagine how scary the sound of that police car was.

I think we must have been holding our collective breath as we listened to the sound of the siren. It seemed like it went on for five or ten minutes. In reality, it was probably half a minute or less and when it was over, I exhaled and then immediately drew in an enormous, deep, breath of recovery.

We may not have been in trouble with the police, but it wasn't long before we felt the wrath of my parents, who may possibly have dealt with us even more harshly than the law.

The siren made us paranoid. We always felt that there might be repercussions from the fight. There never were and in fact we ended up becoming friends with all those lads! I know it sounds weird, but once we got to know each other, there were no problems between us at all, as we realised we were all the same. Our skin colour may have been different and we might speak a different language occasionally but otherwise we were just like all the other local teens, trying to have fun and get on with our lives.

The paranoia meant I couldn't help myself but confide in one of my uncles to tell him about the fight. I was too worried about getting into serious trouble. But it wasn't long before the story got back to my parents and then I really was in trouble. My uncle shared the story with my dad while they were drinking kava one evening, and as calm as the strong herbal drink kept him, the next day me, Mako and Maka all got hidings for fighting. It was the ultimate irony.

'What?' I protested before the punishment was served up. 'It was self-defence.'

My parents weren't interested in any defence plea. I felt it was a bit harsh on us, but they wanted to teach us a lesson. There was a reason why we were always supposed to brush off any racist abuse in our adopted country. My mum and dad felt we had to understand that it was hard for locals to accept different people potentially taking their turf. We're humans, we're all animals and we're territorial. I found it incredibly tough as a child to let stuff like that go. I was always incensed by the injustice of it. But my parents urged us to walk away and turn the other cheek, and after that hiding, we always left it.

There's no doubt my dad was a tough disciplinarian. I think you might have worked that out by now. And he readily admits he was probably too tough on us, not with the hidings so much, but more specifically with the intense training regime he put us under, in order to make sure we were fit enough to become professionals.

From the minute he made us do that brutal winter hill run back in Pontypool when there was a blizzard blowing, when we were just small children and when my mum was screaming at him for being crazy – from that exact minute, we were destined to become international rugby players.

That was the moment that he chose to show us how much hard work was necessary to make it to the top of the game. And given we were also large kids, he wanted to make sure our fitness was never in question so he would make us run regularly. The harder we trained, the more likely it was that we would be able to win when it came to playing matches. That's how Sione would psyche up my dad and the boys before a match, motivating them to go out and be victorious. 'We can win this!' he would urge them, no matter what the odds stacked against them.

'How?' my dad would ask.

'Because of the way you guys train.'

For my dad, the satisfaction of watching us grow into rugby players didn't come when we earned our pro contracts, won major trophies, or made our international debuts although of course he was delighted for us in those moments. My dad's real joy came from watching us complete the toughest training sessions with him. By succeeding in our tasks in those sessions, he knew we were destined to then reap the rewards on the pitch in the years that followed.

Which is all well and good to hear about now, but wasn't much help to me when I was being flogged to death with endless, vomit-inducing running.

As I got older, I would protest and tell him that I didn't need to do the running, that I was perfectly fit enough. His response was that he would watch me play for the school on a Friday and my club on a Sunday, and if I could show him that I was playing well enough for the whole of both games then he would agree that I was fit and didn't need extra training.

The problem with that, of course, was his version of what playing well enough for the whole game was compared to my version.

He came to the games, and felt that there were times when I looked like I didn't really want to be there and that my attitude wasn't right and, in his opinion, that was as a result of a lack of fitness. Or possibly just me having a bad attitude. But it might well have been fitness and that was something he could help me with.

We ran after we returned from school, probably five days a week – as long as I hadn't been sent home or suspended. In Bristol, we had a huge sports pitch right behind our house. It was two pitches actually, one for rugby and one for football, and it must have been around 800 metres all the way round and every afternoon we had to do ten laps followed by sprints.

I'd sit in lessons every day, thinking how much I was not looking forward to running after school. As the clock ticked closer to 3pm, I knew that in around fifteen minutes I'd be running. Almost every other kid would be willing that clock to hit 3pm so they could get out of class, but I would be sitting there willing time to slow right down to delay the inevitable. I was the only school kid in the country who never wanted lessons to end. I'd have happily sat there for the rest of the day if it meant I didn't have to run.

It didn't matter that my dad's running drills were designed to help us become great rugby players. His plan was to make sure that we were the type of player who would have the stamina and fitness to always be wherever the ball was. Whatever else anyone would say about our games in the future, there was no way my dad was going to allow them to question our fitness levels. Not while we were living under his roof at any rate.

But the problem for me was that I absolutely hated running. It was torture. The endless step after step, lap after lap, day after day, week after week. Get me on a rugby pitch and I'd run all day, but the simple act of running for the sake of running was not for me.

Dad was somehow convinced that those laps around the sports pitches were only 400 metres whereas I was certain it was closer to double that. Not that it mattered because we were doing it anyway. What's more, there was a little hill that led down from one pitch to the other, which is all well and good when you're running down it and you need a little boost but a total nightmare when you're coming back up from the other direction.

The only thing that softened the blow was that I ran with the gang which sometimes made everything a bit more bearable and occasionally fun. Me, Mako, Maka, and sometimes Toby and Josh when they moved to Bristol, were all in it together, so we'd try to help each other get through it the best we could under my dad's ever watchful eye.

Sometimes, he would send us out to run and leave us to it, only coming back into the field to tell us when it was time to stop. On those occasions, we would all run with one ear on the sound of the gate into the field. That old gate made a hell of a squeaky racket every time it was opened. So as we were running, if we heard that noise, we'd turn to the gate, half-praying to see my dad telling us we'd done enough. The disappointment was immense when we'd turn to find it was just a random local walking their dog.

It would always begin the night before. When we were praying together as a family at dinner, on top of all the usual stuff like, 'Billy, we got another letter from your school today,' my dad would also say, 'When you get home from school tomorrow, put on your trainers because we're going running.'

Even worse was when he'd spring a surprise session on us. Occasionally, we'd go to school thinking there was no running that day because he hadn't mentioned it the night before. He might have been too busy with work so we were saved. Happy days.

I'd be at home, relaxing in front of the telly when suddenly the phone would ring and my heart would sink. Everyone would stare at the phone in fear, but there was no avoiding the menace of its ringing.

I'd pick up and say, 'Hello?'

'Get your trainers on, we're running when I get home.'

And that was it. The executioner had spoken and we were all on death row, awaiting the sealing of our fate.

That was just the basics. That was your run of the mill, everyday training we had to do that didn't involve a rugby ball at any stage. When the competition stepped up, we had to follow suit. My dad made absolutely sure of that. So when I was lucky enough to be selected for the England

Under-18s training squad at the age of fifteen, my initial elation and joy soon turned sour when my dad introduced me to his premium running drills, tailor-made for his sons who were selected for England. He's finally accepted that he doesn't need to do this anymore as we have clubs that look after our fitness every day, but those were different times back in Bristol.

His main concern was that we were at a disadvantage to the rest of the England boys, because most of them were already part of club academies where their fitness would be regularly assessed and improved where necessary. We might have had all the skills and little touches which looked nice, but my dad felt strongly that our overall aerobic fitness would let us down.

If I wanted to carry the ball at a higher level, I needed to be way more explosive. Likewise with stopping an opponent, or catching a high ball when you're exhausted towards the end of the game. The bottom line was that I needed to be fit enough to do all those things again and again at any stage of the game. And in order to do that, my dad had to make me run more than I had ever run at any stage of my life. And if you understand how much I had already run until that point, you will appreciate that for those few weeks before I joined the England camp, I led an utterly terrifying existence of running followed by running followed by more running. And after that? Running. If at any point I might have thought the running was over, there would definitely be more running. At times, I stopped thinking because I was too busy running. In fact, by the time I got to that England gathering, it was a miracle I could stand up, never mind run.

A standard session of my dad's at this time would begin with the ten laps of the pitches as a warm-up. For most people that wouldn't have been a warm-up, that would have been the whole frigging workout. Not for my dad. Not when his son was wanted by England.

After the warm-up, I would then do eight rounds of 800m with about a minute's rest in between each one. At least he said it was 800m. I was convinced it was a lot closer in distance to 1500m.

Following that, it would be four lots of 400m then two lots of 200m.

Finished? Not even close.

It was then time to go back up with another four lots of 400m and the grand finale of eight sets of 800m which, the more I think about it, were definitely way more like 1500m. By the time I was on those last few rounds of 800m, I was a dead man walking. There is no way you could describe what I would be doing then as running. It was somewhere between walking and running. Somewhere between life and death. Somewhere between the conscious and the unconscious. Somewhere between heaven and hell. Somewhere between a massive rock, and the hardest of all the hard places. That's exactly where I was.

During that build up to my call-up, I wouldn't necessarily do that session every time, although I did it enough times so that it, and the associated pain, is etched into my memory forever. Sometimes, my dad would say we're doing a fifty-five run after the usual warm-up laps. Fortunately, that wasn't another fifty-five circuits of the sports pitches. That would have actually killed me. Instead, it was five full lengths of the pitch without a break, then four full lengths, all the way down to one and back up again. It may not have been as far as the madness of the 800m, 400m and

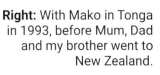

Right: With Mako in Tonga in 1993, before Mum, Dad and my brother went to New Zealand.

Below: Mako, Ana and me in Disneyland in 1999.

Right: Back in Tonga, with Mako. It's 1997 and I'm five.

Right: Year Two at school.

Left: Year Five's 'most improved player', and I was made school captain for the following year.

Below and right: At an Australian zoo on a visit to see family in 2003. With my cousin Chris Talakai (below).

First time I ever had a proper injury. I played through it, but it turned out I had broken my ankle. England Under-18s versus Australia Schools in December 2009.

Playing for England Under-18s against Scotland in April 2010.

My debut for Wasps, versus Harlequins in Abu Dhabi, January 2011. Harrow School didn't know about it!

Wasps versus Saracens, February 2012. It felt weird playing against my brother later that year. I would be joining him at Sarries before too long.

Second game of the season, September 2012, versus Bath.

Above: May 2015. One of my most memorable games. Saracens at Northampton Saints in the Premiership play-off semi-final. We'd lost to them the year before in the last minute.

Above: Our first trophy together, after losses to Toulon and Saints. Mako and me with the Premiership trophy after beating Bath.

Left: December 2015. I manage to get over for the bonus-point try versus Newcastle Falcons. I was best man at Josh's wedding the night before. Nigel Wray kindly flew me and my brother to the game.

An amazing feeling: lifting the European Champions Cup trophy with my brother, after chasing it for so long with Saracens. We beat Racing 92 in Lyon, May 2016.

This photo is so cool. I remember losing two finals in 2014, and thinking how cool it would be to win trophies. I so wished I could win one. With Mako and both the European Champions Cup and Aviva Premiership trophies, Twickenham, May 2016.

It was amazing to achieve another final victory, this time the European Champions Cup against Clermont-Auvergne at Murrayfield, May 2017. Always great to have Mum, Dad and my little cousins there.

My England debut, versus Argentina in Salta, June 2013. Before I came on, I thought my heart was going to jump out of my chest. So great to score, though!

England versus Ireland at Twickenham, February 2014. I was struggling all week with diarrhoea, then landed awkwardly and twisted my ankle. It just wasn't the right time for me. I asked God that day: Why me?

Scoring a try against France at Twickenham, March 2015. Another one of those games in which I wondered whether I'd ever win something with England, after consecutive second-place finishes in the Six Nations.

Great to start the 2016 Six Nations campaign with a win over Scotland at Murrayfield. It was a memorable tournament for all of us. With Chris Robshaw, James Haskell and the Calcutta Cup.

With Eddie Jones after finally breaking a very physical Italian team in Rome, February 2016.

The culmination of so many close games.

Above: With skipper Dylan Hartley and the RBS Six Nations trophy, Paris, March 2016.

Left: Scoring a try against Australia in Sydney, June 2016.

What a great group of lads we have. The England team is such a fantastic place to be every day. Such an honour to represent such an amazing country.

200m, but with no breaks during each set, it was hard enough in its own way and not that friendly to people like me, who enjoy normal breathing patterns.

Whatever the session, we'd normally begin at around 3.30pm – giving me a paltry half-hour break after school to basically go home and get changed into my kit and trainers – and we'd never finish until it was dark. I couldn't even see where I was running by the time the session was over, not that you could describe what I was doing as running anyway.

By the time I turned up at that England training camp, I probably could've represented my adopted country in the marathon. The rugby, however, was a different story and I still needed to work on that.

Occasionally, all the running would get the better of me. Like the time when our Bristol Under-17s team had reached a regional final that was going to be played at Worcester. I hadn't played or trained much at the time, because I was recovering from surgery during which a really painful cyst had been removed from under my armpit. It was grim, and it meant no contact sport for a while. Or running. That was the only silver lining on the cloud.

Once I'd recovered fully, there was still time for me to make it back to full fitness for the final – but that meant it was time for another ruinous running regime. Not just that, but I was doing all the sessions with my dad by myself, because the other boys were as fit as they needed to be and didn't require any extra work. My mission was to catch up with them, but no matter how much I ran, I just wasn't feeling it. Or rather I *was* feeling it. It was too much for me.

One afternoon, my dad marked out another 200m that needed to be sprinted on repeat. It was clearly more like 400m, but he wasn't bothered about that. I certainly was.

'Sprint!' instructed my dad, so off I went.

Except I wasn't exactly powering through the 200m. I ran with the operated arm held against my side on purpose, so that it was impossible for me to really go full throttle. There was nothing whatsoever wrong with that arm, but that wasn't the point. This was my way of showing my dad that I was not prepared to keep running – not if my arm, which had only been in surgery just weeks before, was really hurting.

'What are you running like that for?' bellowed my dad from fifty metres away.

I just carried on running, but by the time I'd got back to the starting point, my dad was fuming.

'My arm's killing me,' I lied.

'Sprint properly! Go!' was his reply. He wasn't interested in my arm. He'd already seen me running normally earlier in the session and there was no way he was falling for any of my crap. I was so angry as I sprinted off, that there were tears in my eyes. This was so unfair, nobody else was doing this. Everyone was hanging out in the park, having a great time except me. I was missing out on all the fun.

The tears started to stream as I turned to sprint back, and I could see Maka walking towards us from the direction of the school and as he got closer, he could see that I was crying and running at the same time. I'd unwittingly invented crunning. But it was no laughing matter at the time.

I made it back to the start again and my dad could see my tear-stained face but he just barked, 'Go! Go! Go!' as I had to do another repetition to complete the set. Maka hurried on home. He didn't want to rubberneck this particular car crash and I didn't blame him for that either.

As always, the pain was only temporary. My tears stopped, the sprints finished and I got to play in the final. I might have hated it at the time but I understand now the importance of that hard work and how it set me up for my future.

I can now look back and say that everyone might have been hanging out in the park while I was getting flogged and bawling my eyes out, but while they're still hanging out some place, I'm the one that's playing at Twickenham for England. That's not me giving it the big 'I am', that's me speaking with the satisfaction of someone who went through a hell of a lot of pain to make it as a professional sportsman.

I also think it must have been so hard for my dad to keep pushing me in the way he did. For starters, my mum was always quarrelling with him about it. She felt that he was asking too much of us with all that running and they used to clash over it. These days, he admits there were times when he pushed me too hard, but I look where I am and I disagree with him. He did what it took to turn me into a rugby player.

But he also didn't have much of a choice in the matter. His upbringing had taught him only one way of doing things and that was the way we also had to do things. If you think my dad was uncompromising when it came to training and rugby, Sione made him look like a puppy.

My dad has five brothers, and all six of them were virtually shoved on to the rugby pitch by Sione. He would never have said this to us as kids, but when he was younger and he found the going got too tough, my dad would feel like giving up. He never wanted to play rugby seriously or even professionally. Once he had his qualification as a quantity surveyor, he felt that's where his focus should be, because he would be able to get far more out of that than he would from rugby, certainly in terms of financial reward.

Dad was ready to leave rugby behind for good and he decided to inform Sione about his decision.

'Dad, I don't want to play rugby,' he said.

'OK, if you don't want to play rugby you can go and look for another house, look for a place to live,' was Sione's matter-of-fact reply.

'What's wrong?' said my dad, but the die had been cast and there was no way Dad could have changed Sione's mind. He might have moaned about it, but when push came to shove, as it often did, he'd be on that rugby pitch, playing his heart out whether it was for the village team or his country.

The amazing thing is that Sione's stubbornness was eventually proved to be absolutely correct and had a direct effect on everything that happened to me and Mako. If my dad had stopped playing rugby, he would never have been in a position to take advantage of the sport turning professional in the UK. And without my dad being in Britain, there is no way Mako or I would've played for England and enjoyed the life we've had here so far. Without rugby, we wouldn't have even been here.

And we needed our dad to push and challenge us, just like Sione had done to him. Once we were around fifteen or sixteen, Dad would always say to us that if we really work and train hard we'd make it as professionals and play at international level. He knew what it took to succeed, and he was convinced we had it and that he could help us by pushing us in the right direction.

For all the moaning I did about running, for my dad it was like hearing an echo of himself from a generation ago. The great irony was that he absolutely detested all that stuff too. The only difference between him and me was that he'd seen the direct benefits of all that training. He'd lived on those benefits. In fact, we'd all lived on them.

But that doesn't mean he also didn't react in the same way I did when he was a kid learning the ropes. When Sione made my dad run and run, my old man's standard response would be, 'Why are we training so hard? Are we playing the All Blacks?' much to the dismay of his father.

He gave his all in every game he played though, never allowing himself to stray too far from the ball, but he was never allowed to show weakness on or off the pitch. This trait started with Sione and was passed down to us by my dad – it probably began way before my grandad but there's nobody around to tell me about those times now.

Sione did not believe in injuries. For him – and therefore eventually for my dad – injuries just weren't a thing. You play the game until it's over and then, if you really have to, you can nurse whatever problem you have before playing again the following week.

When my dad made his debut for our village team Toa Ko Maafu, he was in for a rude awakening. Local rugby in Tonga is rough. And when I say rough, it's completely indisciplined with mayhem going on everywhere you look, and in most places you don't look. Back home, if someone wants to bang you on the rugby pitch they won't wait for a more subtle opportunity like a ruck. Instead, they'll boldly walk up to you in the middle of the game and hit you, no questions asked, and no matter what's actually happening on the pitch at that particular moment. It's like the Wild West out there.

During one of his first games, my dad got hurt during a scrum. He went down on the pitch clutching his neck, clearly in pain. Sione was watching on the sidelines and was mightily unimpressed.

'Hey! Get up!'

That wasn't the end of the lack of sympathy. It was actually just the beginning.

'If you ever go down holding your neck again, I'll come and break it myself!'

The way my dad tells it, he was still in agony with his hands clasped round his neck for support at the time. Not that it made any difference to his dad.

'Go and break it then! I'll go to the shop and buy you a new one tomorrow!'

'Gosh!' thought my dad. 'That's my dad saying that!'

When that's the message you're getting, it's little wonder that my dad's attitude to weakness or injury is most politely described as impatient. It's the kind of attitude that would've been irritated by my armpit cyst, and utterly uninterested in my feeble and dishonest complaints about the pain coming from my arm while I ran.

It's also the kind of attitude which makes him strongly believe that certain injuries are not actually injuries at all. For example, occasionally I would pick up one of those permanent dead legs which can take a few days to heal and are really quite painful. So I would explain that I had a dead leg and my dad's response was, 'That's not an injury.'

'All right, it *is* an injury, but . . .'

'No, I don't think that's an injury'.

OK, Dad. You know best. Even better than doctors and surgeons, apparently. During a 2016 Test against Argentina, I somehow managed to tear the cartilage in my right knee. I could barely stand on that leg, and had to leave the field on one of those embarrassing medical carts they drive on to the pitch for such occasions. The following day I had a scan which confirmed the problem, and that was immediately followed by surgery to repair the cartilage, after which my dad got in touch.

'Why did you have surgery?' he asked.

'Errr . . . because my meniscus had flipped inside,' was my clinical reply.

'Nah, you could've rehabbed it without surgery,' Dr Vunipola came back at me.

'Mate, the surgeon who studied for around ten or fifteen years is telling me I needed surgery, and you're telling me I don't?'

'I'm telling you, you would've been fine,' said my dad, and that was the end of that. Except I'd had the surgery, so we'll never know if he was right. I suspect he was probably wrong on that particular occasion, but he was right about most things.

Especially all that flipping running.

7

Fat and Homeless

I feel like an absolute clown. And I look like one too, so it's no wonder I feel one.

This is England, Billy. England! And look at the state of me.

I know what everyone's thinking. I can feel all those eyes on me. They're all judging me. And they're all spot on. I'm a total mess.

This is England and I'm a total mess.

They can see that. They're not stupid.

My heart is racing, pumping and stomping all over the place.

I'm with the big boys now. I am a big boy myself, but I'm with the real big boys now. The top dogs. The daddies. The finest in the land.

We're still kids – I'm a real kid – all of us in our teens but we're here to represent England. Or at least to see if we can represent England.

I've heard about these boys. I can't look them in the eye. I try to catch cheeky glimpses of them when they're not looking at me, which is hard because they're all looking at me.

I'm the new kid. I'm only fifteen and I'm here at the Aztec West hotel in Bristol with the Under-18s.

I didn't have far to travel. Not in terms of miles on the day. But, in reality, I've come so far to be here. That's what I'm thinking as I sit here.

As I sit here surrounded by these giants.

I'm bigger than the lot of them, but they're the giants.

I'm the kid from Tonga. It's a long way from my village Longo Longo to Bristol's Aztec West hotel. I've no idea how far it is, but it's probably further than anyone else here has travelled today.

I'm looking down and I remember the state of me. Because I can see the state of my kit. What am I doing here?

What am I doing here, sitting with Owen Farrell and George Ford, boys who I've already heard so much about?

What am I doing here, wearing a pair of worn-out boots with holes in that my uncle once gave me, that are still wet from the game I played for my Sunday League team last weekend? And then there's my Canterbury rugby top that has rips all over it, mainly because Josh, Toby, Mako and me have all shared it when we play our two-on-two games against each other. It's not doing a great job of covering my belly.

And the cherry on the icing on the cake, are my shorts, more merchandise from those garden games which are now so small for me that I've had to use scissors to cut each side, so that I'm now somehow squeezed into them.

The sum total of the look is more fat and homeless than England star of the future.

Farrell and Ford look immaculate, I see when I catch them off guard for a second. The kit is ironed, fresh and new or nearly new. They play for academy teams at some of the best clubs in the country.

My mum did iron my kit last night, for what it was worth bless her, but I play for my local comprehensive school in Bristol and a Sunday team. There's no comparison.

But here I am. Here's the guy who everyone thinks is fat and homeless sitting on the same benches as the England players. I'm on their level, but I'm feeling like I barely belong here.

This is England and I barely belong here.

● ● ●

We move out to the training pitch.

My heart's still going bananas and my boots are still wet. Farrell and Ford's boots are bone dry and probably feel like they're about to play in their slippers.

They're involved in the first drills and I'm not.

I'm watching and I'm bricking it.

They're probably all staring at me from the pitch.

On the other side of the pitch, I see the coach Peter Walton talking to Charlotte, the team manager. She says some stuff to him and he walks over to me.

I'm thinking this could go one of two ways. He is either going to ask me something about rugby, or he's going to find out what on earth this fat and homeless guy is doing at an England training session.

As he approaches, I suck in some air. I need it.

'Billy, have you ever thought about playing prop?'

I kind of give him a look in my eyes that says, 'No, and don't even think about it', but fortunately when my brain engages I only manage to offer a verbal 'No.'

He seems quite happy with that answer. He doesn't follow up with anything persuasive designed to convince me that doing all that donkey work is a good idea.

I think this guy respects me. I feel warmth and respect back for him immediately.

All of this is done without any further verbal communication, but we don't need it. Peter and I are going to get on.

Soon, I get on. To the pitch for my first drills as a potential England player.

Suddenly, I feel like I want this badly and I don't want to make a mess of it. I want to grasp it, feel it and never let it go. I want to wear that shirt more than anything else in the world. I really want to show these guys what I can do. Because I know I can do it. Even though I'm terrified of all of them, of being here, of all their kit and everything else, I want to impress them.

We're doing a move, I'm told by one of the coaches. I don't know what a move is. I've got some moves that I use for certain tunes I like to listen to with the boys, but I don't think they're going to come in handy here.

It turns out that this move is a starting move we're going to rehearse. The coach says that if the scrum is on the left side of the pitch, then we have to hit the middle of the pitch and keep going the same way, if that's the call. And if there's another call, then we go left to the scrum. He tells us the words which mean go right or left, but I can't take it all in. He's talking a lot and I'm finding it hard to work out what to do.

I'm nervous as hell, so I can't focus enough. But I'm doing a good impression of someone who is very focused.

'Everyone OK with that?' asks the coach.

'Yeah, sweet,' I reply, as everyone else nods, and then I'm doing the drill, and I'm running right but everyone's going left. I'm angry with myself, they're all looking at me again like I'm some kind of clown. And I am.

Then, I get it wrong again.

And again.

I turn to my right and ask Sam Jones what the call they keep using actually means and he whispers, 'Same way! Same way!' and next time I get it right. And the time after that. Thanks Sam. Sam's the man.

And suddenly I'm more relaxed and I'm almost enjoying it, even if I do look like a total mug in my awful gear. Because this is England. And it seems to be going OK.

Even though I'm doing a load of loose stuff and not really following everything, I'm getting encouragement from coaches and some of the boys. They tell me there's a trial match against South West Academies – some of the top kids from Bath, Bristol and Exeter will be playing against us and I'm going to be involved. I know this is my chance and I know I have to take it. I try not to think about it as it comes around fast.

● ● ●

I'm on the pitch, ready to start the game. I've got some half-decent kit on. Not the England shirt but some better gear than the stuff I've been training in for the last few days.

We're poised for kick-off. I'm ready for this.

I can feel the adrenaline surge, mixed with that nervous energy, both rocketing through my veins and making me feel pumped up but a little sick at the same time.

I'm not going to let this opportunity go. No way. But I need to stay relaxed despite everything I can feel happening in my body.

Calm down.

The referee looks around the pitch. He's probably counting the players or something. No need for that, I'm here and I'm ready.

Calm down.

We're kicking off and we have a kick-off plan. I go through it in my head. It's going up high and I'm going to chase it down. I'm going to run as fast as I can and I'm not going to stop until I've got it.

Calm down.

The ref blows his whistle. I look up and the ball is sailing through the air. It's high, it's handsome and I'm on the move. I'm tearing after it like one of those dogs in the field, the ones who might have watched me struggling through all those runs my dad has been making me do.

But I'm not struggling now. I'm flying.

Calm down.

The ball's dropping and I'm about ten metres away from it. If the kid underneath it just stays put and catches it, there's not a great deal I can do other than show my intention. For next time. And there will be a next time.

Calm down.

I'm got my eye on the ball and the kid. And the kid is jumping for it, he's on the move right now so I can do something here. He's up in the air and he's got it. Now, gravity is doing its thing and he's about to land back down on the pitch with the ball clutched safely in his arms.

But there's nothing safe about it, because if I've timed this right, I'm going to be there at the exact same time he drops. I swear there must be a God. This is why I believe in God. This is too perfect. He must have arranged this for me.

This is it. This is my moment.

The kid lands and I arrive at that exact moment and I steam straight through him and write him off. It's a tough one for him, but it's a special moment for me.

This is the end of my beginning. This is England and I belong. I want to be an England player. I'm going to be an England player. I'm going to be neither fat nor homeless.

● ● ●

OK, so I was never homeless. Not with my amazing parents supporting me. But I might well have been fat for a while longer, despite my best intentions. At 142kg, I had a huge amount of work to do.

Whenever I was with the Under-18s, I'd always go for an afternoon sleep because I do love a kip but also because that training was a different level to what I was used to. Frankly, I was absolutely knackered after chasing people like Owen Farrell around all morning. I always asked for a snack to eat before I went to sleep, exactly as I would do at home, but I was told that it wasn't healthy to eat before lying down and going to sleep. Peter Walton and the England experts tried to educate me about nutrition, but it would take a few more years for that particular penny to drop.

Not that I wasn't willing to learn. I had to be when I was in that set-up. It was the most exciting thing that had ever happened to me and it made me hungry to make it to the very top. All I had needed was a tiny sniff or a taste of what could be – and that had first come via my brother the year before me.

Mako was also called up to the Under-18s (not when he was fifteen, but let's not get competitive) and went on a tour to Argentina with them which must have been unreal for him. For me, it made me desperate to follow in his footsteps. Before moving to Bristol, I had never considered playing for England as an option. Even Wales seemed unlikely.

But when Mako returned from his first training camp with that indescribable glow that I could sense but never understand until a year later, I suddenly had to play for England no matter what. In that uniquely adolescent way, it instantly became one of the most important things in my life, after my family.

Given our humble rugby gear collection, I remember the first thing I said to him when he returned from that get together.

'Wow, did you get kit?' I asked with the widest of wide eyes.

'Will you shut up?' came my brother's totally expected, no-nonsense response.

He definitely played it like someone who was never interested in material stuff like that. Even if he was, there was no way he would ever admit that to his little brother. But that attitude works well alongside mine. He tapered everything and kept expectations down which was a solid antidote to some of my over-the-top, boyish enthusiasm.

In 2008 I received an invite to an England summer training camp for the first time, but thanks to an extremely poorly-timed infection I was unable to take part which was such a blow.

A few months later, Mako and I both received letters in the post from the RFU – yes, the actual England Rugby Football Union. My parents opened Mako's first and he had been invited to be part of the Under-18 squad again which was no surprise after the previous year.

Then they opened my letter. I was fifteen. There was no expectation at all, other than all the hopes and dreams which I had carried since Mako's first experience the year before and then transported through my illness in the summer. In other words, there were overflowing, bucket-loads of expectation.

It didn't take long before I read my dad's facial expression and realised I was in. The funny thing was that my first thought wasn't that instant elation I would've expected. In fact, it was a rather prescient notion about exactly what that meant for me and my life for the next few weeks.

'Oh crap,' I thought. 'My dad's gonna frigging drill me!'

And I was so right.

'Right Billy,' said my dad. 'We're happy for you, but you're obviously nowhere near that team yet . . .' He left that one hanging as my worst fears were realised, and we soon began that endless series of brutal running sessions.

I was desperate for some new moulded boots before joining up with

England, but my dad couldn't find any in my size. My feet were huge so that was always a problem. But so was money. Mako was at Millfield at the time which is a private school, but I didn't really appreciate what that meant then. Instead of the mouldeds, my dad presented me with some astroturfs he'd managed to find in my size. My reaction was to burst into tears.

'It's fine! It's fine!' he said.

'Dad,' I sobbed. 'I can't wear those, everyone's gonna think I'm a mug.' It's laughable now, but the importance of those things to me at the time was off the scale.

Despite all that anxiety, and having to go to the camp on my own because Mako couldn't make it, I was pretty confident in my ability at that stage. I'd been playing number eight for a while and knew what I could do, so I had no hesitation in declining Peter Walton's prop invitation.

Once I settled in, I was running everywhere and flying into challenges. Every time I had an opportunity to run at someone one-on-one I'd try my hardest, and every time someone ran at me, I'd try to hit them as hard as I could. And that was just in training because that was my mindset then. I was a bit like a Duracell battery, except I'd eventually run out. I also still massively lacked game understanding, but I started to work stuff out a bit more after a while.

More games against other academy sides followed, so I must have done enough to impress in that initial trial game against South West Academies, despite the very close attention of my cousin Anthony Maka, who was in the opposition that day. He kept going after me, time and again, so I just said to him, 'Mate, what are you doing? Go and tackle someone else!'

'They told me to come and get you,' he replied.

'Are you serious?' I asked him, amazed that I could be targeted like that, especially by one of my boys.

Before I knew it, I was sat on the bench for my first international match against Scotland in a game played up in Newcastle. Unfortunately, my parents couldn't be there as I think it was too pricey for them to get up to the north east. They missed a special show as we won 63–0 and I just remember being so emotional about the whole experience. I stood next to my brother to sing the national anthem, and while I was sitting on the bench I couldn't stop thinking, 'I've made it, I've made it!', but of course I hadn't.

Having said that, it was an extraordinary bunch of players in that Under-18 squad. Among the guys to start that day were Manu Tuilagi, Jonathan Joseph and Christian Wade, as well as Ford and Farrell, obviously. Peter Walton told me recently that only two of that group haven't played in the Premiership and more than half of us went on to become England Saxons or full internationals.

They must have rated us, because Walts and Neil Taylor used to come and visit Mako and I every fortnight. These weren't social trips but training sessions in Thornbury Park, where the coaches' RFU pads, cones and balls would be put out alongside the kids eating ice creams, and dog-owners with their pooper scoopers picking up their charges' waste.

It was hardly the most glamorous setting – you certainly don't get that at Pennyhill Park – but it was fun because the guys made it that way. It was usually me, Mako, and Toby Faletau too – Toby being trained by England is funny to think about now that he plays for Wales, but it didn't make a difference to Walts and Neil. It must have been a hell of a sight for the locals in the park, as us three monsters were put through our paces by the England coaches.

They always tried to make the sessions fun, because they knew we had no real passion for fitness or running drills. Dad had definitely made that impossible. But they were tough too. We did lots of sprints, shorter distances than my dad made us run but we did them much faster. They made them into games, but as soon as we were doing it, I remember thinking, 'Gosh, this is not much fun at all,' as we never stopped moving for a second. Once I'd moved to Harrow, Neil even came there to work with me as the school stopped playing rugby after December. Those were one-on-one sessions which killed me and I spent most of them saying, 'Mate, give me a break!' but I really appreciate them now.

Walts always said that one of the things he liked about me at the time was my competitive streak. I had to win at all costs, second place was not acceptable. My refusal to accept defeat certainly played out during two games for the Under-18s against Australia and South Africa when I picked up bad injuries but insisted on staying on the pitch. Back then, I couldn't really play more than forty-five or fifty minutes of a game without having to come off. I'd give it everything I had for that time, but then I'd slowly start to fade, because I was just too fat. And you wonder why they wanted me to work on my fitness and nutrition.

We went out to South Africa to play against their Under-18s and I hurt my ankle really badly after only a few minutes. They tried to get me to come off but I refused as I thought my team needed me. I stayed on the pitch and ended up having to wear a protective boot for eight weeks after that game.

Then, when we were playing against Australia at Sale in another youth Test, I turned my ankle early on and it was incredibly sore. I could barely stand on it without wanting to scream out in pain. I started walking around, hoping it would ease off and remembering Sione's philosophy that in a worst case scenario my dad could always buy me a new ankle.

The team physio came on to the pitch to see what the problem was and was fairly up front with me. 'Just man up and run! If not, get off!'

I didn't want to let the team down by coming off, so I started running around as much as I could. I couldn't show weakness. Except my insides were doubled-up in pain.

What was actually happening was that the ligament, the one that holds the two bones together that go down the leg to the ankle, was splitting every time I took a step. By then, I was training with Wasps and when they had a look at it the following day, they wanted me to have surgery on it.

But that's when my dad, Dr Vunipola, stepped in. On this occasion, he was there in time to prevent surgery, insisting that the injury could be healed with simple rehab. And you know what? He was right. So much so, that medics now think twice about surgeries for those types of injury.

I didn't stay on those pitches to play through the pain specifically for

Walts. I did it for everyone around me, him included. You can say it was stupid and I couldn't argue with that assessment. After all, there is no point making an injury worse, as it might mean you have to wait longer until you're fit enough to play again. But I don't think like that. I think about not showing weakness and being responsible for those around me. It's my culture and it's something the England guys had to work out to get the best out of me, which is something at which Walts, and the amazing team manager Charlotte Gibbons, excelled.

Walts has since told me that he knew I was going to play for England from the first time he saw me play, aged fifteen. That's a big call, but I have no doubt he was being sincere when he said that. He knew there were people who doubted me, those who thought my attitude wasn't right because I could appear a bit aloof and lazy. Those same people thought my size was going to be a problem too. They said I was too fat to make it. Fortunately, Peter Walton was not one of those people and was convinced by me immediately.

He never told me all that back then, but what he did do was explain to me that I should never expect to be picked. If I had the attitude that I was going to make the team, then there was a very good chance that I would find myself not included in it. This was quite a hard concept for me to grasp. Not because I was cocky – even though I definitely was then – but because I had grown up learning to expect to be picked in every team. It was very hard to unlearn that. And not just that, I would probably be the captain of the team. And not just that, I would probably be asked to play for the team two years older than me too. I had just got used to things coming easy to me my whole life when it came to rugby, so to change that way of thinking was not natural or straightforward.

Walts also knew which buttons to press to get me going. He'd offer to show me videos of other players, either opponents or senior players I could learn from, but I was never really into that. My line was always that I would go out there and try to be the best I could possibly be on the day. I was far more into focusing on my own game and helping my team that way. That's not to say I couldn't learn from other players, because I certainly could and still continue to do so. Walts respected that and he also bought in to the fact that my motivations were probably not going to be the same as everyone else's. If there were times when I was struggling for whatever reason, he'd pull me to one side and say, 'Come on mate, what's all this for?'

'I want to make my family proud,' was my simple answer.

'Well, come on then . . .,' he urged.

It was simple but it was so true. As a Tongan, that's exactly what we're all about and I was no different. Everything I do, I do to make my family proud, nowhere more so than on the rugby pitch. That was always my main motivation. It wasn't about the financial side of things, it was much more about where we come from. To play for England at any level, having come from a tiny village in Tonga, where the entire country's population is 107,000, to a country with more than 60 million people, means that I am representing my original country in the best possible light. That was the best motivation for me.

I never needed a coach to say, 'See that guy on the other team, he said you were ugly,' or 'That guy said he was way better than you'. I couldn't care less about that, but my family and our heritage is one of the most important things to me.

So before I was going out to play an Under-18 game, Walts would come up to me and say, 'You're doing this for your family today.' I already knew that. He already knew that I knew. But hearing those words from someone else reinforced it for me and just got me that extra bit pumped up, whether I needed to be or not.

Charlotte was also so helpful to me at that time. Walts always said she was like a second mum to us and I think he was right. I also think she must have felt really sorry for me, especially on that first day when I couldn't have been more of a fish out of water if I'd turned up in an empty aquarium. I can imagine her looking at me with pity – 'Oh, look at him with his ripped shorts and his holes in his boots.'

That pity must have worked because she's always looked out for me and gone above and beyond the call of duty by doing things like driving me up and down the motorway to training camps and games when I was at Harrow. The cool thing is Charlotte has progressed with me, Mako and everyone else from that team, as she now has the same role with the senior team.

From the early days, I think the main reason why she always looked out for me – other than pity – is because she was also worried about me. I think she thought I was a bit loose and needed taking care of. She knows that I'm the kind of guy who might not fully think about stuff before I do it. And despite all the evidence staring me in the face from my past, part of me still thinks that's probably the best way to be. Just get on with life and don't spend too much time worrying about stuff. Because that's never come back to bite me on the bum, has it?

● ● ●

I look up and I see red.

Not only a red mist, which I'm definitely seeing but another red.

The colour of the card is red and it's pointing at me.

Oh crap.

What have I done?

Why have I done this?

Why do I always do these stupid things?

OK, this is just a school match, but I've just come back from training with England and this is not going to go down well.

Everyone knows I've just been with England. My team-mates. The opposition. The referee certainly knows. But for some reason I seem to have forgotten.

I should really know better.

I should not be behaving like this.

What did I do? What did I say?

I can still only see red, even though I'm now walking off the pitch.

There's a red filter covering everything I can see.

The pitch is red. The people on the sidelines are red. The clouds in the sky are red. My rugby teacher Lloyd Spacey is red in the face.

But the irony is that I'm being sent off for turning the air blue.

I swore at the ref, who, to be fair, I haven't left alone for the majority of the game and it's not even half-time yet.

What is the matter with me? Why do I do these things?

Once I stop seeing red, I see my future. And I see my dad.

He's not at the game, but he's definitely going to feature in my next few hours once he hears about this.

I've let him down. I've let the whole family down and I've certainly let Spacey and my team-mates down.

I started the game wondering what the hell I was doing wasting my time playing for the school when I've just been representing my country. Now I'm not even able to play for the school, never mind my country. I'm such a fool.

Maybe my dad won't find out. Maybe I can keep this from him? That's what I'll do. I just won't tell him.

● ● ●

I'm heading home now. My dad will ask me how the game was and I'll tell him we won and it was good. I'll tell him the referee was annoying, in case he hears anything about me and the ref. That should do it.

We won the game and it was good. We won the game and it was good.

That's all I can hear as I open the door and walk into the house.

We won the game and it was good.

My dad's standing there, as if he was waiting for me to get home.

We won the game and it was good.

He looks angry.

We won the game and it was good.

He knows.

We won the game and it was good.

'What on earth are you doing swearing at the ref?' he says.

I don't say a word. We won the game and it was good.

'Have you not learned?'

We won the game and it was good.

'You're fifteen, you should've learned by now.'

We won the game and it was good.

How did he know? How does he always know?

Spacey must have called him to tell him what happened.

Spacey. Supposed to be on my side. Supposed to be looking out for me. But rats on me to my dad when I get a red card so now I'm getting a hiding.

Thanks Space.

My dad smashes me for a bit. It hurts, but it's normal. I'm used to it.

I grit my teeth. Show no weakness. He can buy me a new neck. There are no injuries so there is no pain.

It's over.

My dad looks at me. What's he going to say now? He never says anything after a hiding, he just walks off.

'Right, you only played forty minutes, go and do a forty-minute run.'

Oh crap.

He never misses a trick.

I've still got to play the second half on my own is what he's saying, just running about with no ball.

So I get a hiding and *I have to run. When will I ever learn? Hang on, that's his line.*

It's already dark outside as I head out on to the street. It's not like I even have an iPod or something to listen to on these runs. That would change everything. But instead I have the voice in my head. It's me. The soundtrack to every run. Me, and the struggle of my lungs to take in enough oxygen to keep going.

He says he'll be waiting outside after forty minutes to tell me when time's up, but I have no idea if this is going to be a real forty minutes or his fantasy forty minutes that's actually more like an hour – a bit like those 200m distances he measures out.

I leave our house which is part of a great, big block of houses, and run about 200m to the end of our road where the school is. An actual 200m, not my dad's 200m.

I carry on past the Thornbury Castle hotel, then turn left. Now, it's 300m in the other direction before I turn left again to run down the high street and complete the rectangle back home.

That's one lap done. I've no idea how long it has taken me, but I know it's not forty minutes. Not because there's no sign of my dad, but because I know that was not even close to forty minutes.

I carry on pounding the streets, bored out of my brains, thinking back to my stupidity with the referee earlier. My big mouth that's making me run right now. I've got to stop doing these things. I've just played for England, enough is enough.

I'm back on the high street again, hopefully for the last time. I feel like I've been going forever. I can nearly see our street.

'Please come out of the house, Dad,' I think.

I'm at the house. No sign of him. Time for another lap.

There's the school.

Now, here's the hotel.

And the high street again. It never ends.

'Please come out.'

But he's still not there and I have to continue.

It must be more than forty minutes. If I'd have kept my big mouth shut and stayed on the rugby pitch, I wouldn't have covered even half this distance. I wouldn't have noticed the fact I was even running because I would've just been lost in the game.

Again, past the school and hotel. Another time on the high street, but this time he has to be there. He has to be.

'Please come out. Please come out.'

There's not a soul outside the house. Not even somebody I could possibly mistake for my dad by accident.

I have to keep running. I'm doing something that's halfway between a walk and a jog, but I can't stop. Not unless my dad tells me time's up.

Maybe it's not been forty minutes yet and this is just my mind playing tricks on me?

Yeah, right. And maybe the referee who sent me off will be waiting outside the school with a kebab for me next time I run past. Same likelihood.

I've done more than twenty laps. This has to end.

I'm on the high street again. If this doesn't end now then I'll . . . I don't know what I'll do. Keep running I suppose.

'Please come out.'

He's not there again. Where the hell is he? This isn't even funny anymore. It wasn't even funny to start with.

When am I going to learn?

● ● ●

After twenty-three laps, my dad was standing outside our house waiting for me. I don't think I've ever been so happy to see him. The cruel irony of me being delighted to see the face of the man who had sent me out on that torturous task was not lost on me.

Was my lesson learned? Probably not. In the long run – absolutely no pun intended – I think I did learn something because I gradually started seeing sense and realised how futile it was to talk back to officials or argue with them. But it still took a while for that to sink in with me. Even after that incident, I would get really fired up with referees, and I continued to harass them while I was still playing schoolboy rugby. I always thought I was right and I was very stubborn so it was a recipe for disaster, and I continued to get into the odd spot of bother on the pitch.

Once, when I was at Harrow School, we actually had Irish referee JP Doyle come to officiate in one of our school games, which was a bit like Pierluigi Collina turning up to referee a Sunday League football match. We were winning but, for some reason, I kept dropping the ball that day, so I started complaining about that to the referee – don't ask me why, it seemed like a good idea at the time.

'You want to get some gloves, mate,' was JP's smart-arse reply.

'You want to get some Premiership games, mate,' I replied as quick-as-a-flash before I'd even had time to think about it.

Some school friends on the sidelines were all laughing their heads off and our coach smirked a bit too but then told them all off for messing around, so I scarpered to the other side of the pitch before I got into trouble. But I just couldn't help myself with things like that. I would act way before a thought had even entered my mind.

Eventually, as I matured, I did understand my dad's point that my mouth would get me and my team into trouble. Does that justify all that running? I think so, but you draw your own conclusions. I'm not here to preach, I'm just telling you how it was.

The truth was playing for England Under-18s at the age of fifteen was an enormous moment for me, but it was something that I let go to my head.

I came back from the training camps, and the international matches, and just felt like school rugby was not really doing it for me anymore. It was hard to be motivated for those games. There might have even been a part of me that felt like those matches were beneath an international like myself. As if I shouldn't have even had to lower myself. And if I was going to do it, the very least I could expect was referees who were going to be competent and see games the way I saw them.

It was a disgusting, embarrassing attitude that sounds awful now and needed to be knocked out of me. Running twenty-three laps of that little rectangle near my house was not pleasant, but it did give me time to reflect. And I could definitely see what an idiot I'd been. But the hardest part was trying not to be like that. I was lucky though. Other people in my position may not have been as fortunate as me, because I had such great people around me – and they helped me to see where I was going wrong, allowing me to eventually shut down any kind of wrong attitude.

There was my dad, of course, who had his own way of successfully shutting down my rebellious side. But people like Lloyd Spacey were amazing as well. He may well have told my dad about the red card, thus scuppering my plans to pretend the incident had never happened, but I realised that he did it for the right reasons. He was behind me, literally, from the moment I smashed him over during our first school rugby session, and was part of a team of people, like Uncle Daws and Tiger, who helped me so much on my journey from Tonga to Twickenham. Even with my crappy kit.

8

My Big Tongan Head

I'm lining up with my team-mates, ready to run on to the pitch and play. But I should be in school. I look around me. I've never been so scared in my life. At least not since the last time I was this scared, but I can't remember when that was. Probably when I cried because I didn't have any clean clothes to change into after that muddy school game in Wales.

I feel a bit like a schoolkid right now. Not just because I actually am, but also because I'm stood alongside some giants of the game, professionals who get paid to play, and tonight I am somehow their equal. Yet I'm looking up to them like a snotty-nosed junior who's visiting the senior school for the first time.

And I'm nervous. Really nervous. My heart feels like it's working so hard that it could actually pop right out of my mouth any second now.

All I can think is that I really should be in school because I'm not supposed to have the weekend off. Yet here I am about to play a pro game for Wasps.

Even thinking that is making me shake inside. All I've ever wanted to do is play rugby professionally and I'm about to make my debut, here, in Abu Dhabi for some reason.

It's not how I would've scripted it, but it's not an opportunity I'm going to turn down. And it's not like when they asked me to play I was going to say 'Nah, I'm alright thanks.'

But I do feel like this is crazy. Here I am in the Middle East about to make my debut for Wasps against our fierce rivals Harlequins.

I look along the line and see guys like Karl Dickson and George Lowe in Quins shirts. 'Oh my gosh!' I think. 'I've watched some of these guys playing on TV. They've all won trophies and stuff. I can't tackle them!'

I'm completely overawed. I can feel it all over.

Abu Dhabi. The crazy luxury of the Emirates Palace Hotel. The flight over here. The LV= Cup match. I've just turned eighteen years old, for goodness sake. Please God, help me!

I'm on the pitch now, ready to start the game. There are still nerves flying all over my body. There must be about 5,000 people here watching me. Not the game, just me.

But this is my dream. This is the moment I've been waiting for. The moment I've worked so hard for. All that flipping running. Come on. Please God, help me!

The whistle blows and I'm running. It's all I can do to calm myself down. I don't even know where I'm running. Where am I running? Please God, help me!

Everything's happening really fast, I'm trying to keep up. It's only been a minute, but I feel like my heart's going to give way if I carry on like this for much longer.

We've got a penalty, I can chill for a bit. Thank God. OK, I need to get into this now. There are cameras everywhere, I notice now, as the penalty sails in between the posts to put us ahead.

The game is on telly, my parents can see me. Everyone can see me. That's pretty cool. 'Hello Mum,' I think, but don't say.

Game's back on. Time to focus. Just be yourself, it'll be fine. Just do your normal thing. It'll be OK. If I can just remember what my normal thing actually is.

But there's no time to think because our scrum-half Nick Berry has the ball and I'm just inside him. He feeds me and I'm off. I'm running with the ball. This is it. I'm running with the ball in a pro rugby game like real pros do. But where on earth am I going? Straight ahead. Straight ahead. Please God, help me!

I'm about to smash into someone so I shut my eyes and hope for the best.

We have impact.

Ouch.

I feel something on my knee and then I'm down. I make the ball available and hear the whistle. Someone else is down next to me. I look up.

I've hit Mark Lambert, the Quins prop. Or to be more accurate, my knee has thudded straight into Mark Lambert's head and he is totally out of it.

Great start, Bill. Not only am I not at all scared to tackle these giants of the game, apparently I'm absolutely fine to put them in an ambulance.

Why me? Please God, help me!

He's going to be OK, I think. The physio is on and he's come round. He's probably really badly concussed and he's leaving the pitch horizontally but he's OK. Which is something, I guess. These things happen. To me.

We're playing and I'm running again. Got to put that accident out of my mind. He's fine. Get on with it. Have fun. Live the dream.

Someone's running at me fast. I try to stop him, but I bounce off him and he's away. What happened? In an Under-18 match, I would've taken the guy out, but this is different. These guys are strong. I'm big, but I'm eighteen. I don't do weights properly. I go to school every day. These guys are doing upper body while I'm doing business studies.

And it shows. Through the pain in my shoulder, it shows. That's another painful hit I've taken right there. It's not even a fair fight.

And that's also the case in the match because we are getting hosed. Quins are tearing us apart. And that hurts too, but it's still so exciting. My heart is pumping like it never has before. I must have been at ninety per cent of my max heart rate for the whole game so far. Is that even possible? It feels like it is.

I hate losing but I might be allowed to enjoy this one. As long as I don't smile in front of the TV cameras, it'll be OK. I can't have anyone at home thinking I'm OK with getting beat. But, just for today, I am.

● ● ●

I still think that trip was wasted on me. Abu Dhabi for a long weekend to play rugby? I didn't realise how good I had it. I had a swimming pool, literally outside my hotel bedroom. I didn't even need to walk around the hotel. Just straight out of my sliding doors and almost into the pool. There were incredible restaurants in this place with some of the best chefs in the world cooking for guests. The grounds of the hotel alone were bigger than my village back in Tonga – that's how the hotel was able to stage our match in a 5,000-seater stadium in its back garden. Every time I clicked a finger, someone would've come running asking me what I wanted. And they would've brought me anything too. Pizza. A burger. A kebab from my favourite Pontypool kebab house. OK, maybe not that one. But, pretty much anything. All that on tap, and so, so much more. And what did I do? I barely left my room the whole time I was there.

I was just way too scared to do anything wrong. As cool as it was to make my pro debut aged eighteen and still at school, I was a kid. I hardly said a word to anyone and took no advantage of the insane luxury of my temporary accommodation.

I'd got the call from Wasps earlier that week. It was an incredible few days. The club was staging this home group match in the cup to raise its profile in the United Arab Emirates. A few regulars were missing and I was asked to make my debut. Usually, that's just an invitation you don't even have to reply to, because it's such an obvious yes. But, in my case, I had to reply by saying something along the lines of 'I'd love to, but I need to ask my teacher,' which is not a sentence that most pros would ever say.

My guy at Harrow School was Jesse Coulson, someone else who has been an invaluable help on my journey. I went with his blessing. As the school's Director of Sport and 1st XV rugby coach, the club would've had to request permission from him, but it's quite possible I never told a number of other key people at Harrow – like the rest of my teachers and masters there. So when I returned, there were a few conversations that went along the following lines:

'Where have you been?'

'Abu Dhabi, playing for Wasps.'

'Why didn't you tell me?'

'Didn't think of it.'

It wasn't arrogance, it was just me. Once it all happened, it happened fast and my head was in a spin so there were people I forgot to tell. One minute, I was studying for my Photography A-Level, and the next I was flying to the Middle East. It was all quite similar to the experience of suddenly joining a school like Harrow after five years at my comprehensive in Bristol which was amazing but just not in the same league.

I was never meant to go to Harrow. My dad had pretty much decided to send me to Millfield, another top private school that was well-regarded for its sports teams. Mako was already there so it made sense. My parents were on the move too, as my mum had landed another job as a minister at a church, this time moving further east to High Wycombe. So they'd go there with my sisters, and Mako and I would board. All of which happened, except I ended up boarding at Harrow after being offered a scholarship quite late in the day.

My dad went off the idea of sending me to Millfield after we went to the open day there. Funnily enough, I felt the exact opposite about it. That day was great as I met loads of people at the school and was really excited about starting there. It was a mixed school, like my school in Thornbury, so I naturally got a few girls' numbers from that visit. I guess I'm just a bit better looking than my brother. On the way back to Thornbury, my dad noticed that I kept receiving text messages and was laughing to myself in the back of the car. He assumed I was already messaging the girls at Millfield, and told my mum, 'It's going to be dangerous sending him to that school,' so when the offer came from Harrow – a boys school – he changed his mind and told me that's where I was going. I wasn't happy, but Harrow was a phenomenal school so it wasn't the end of the world.

When we went to visit my new school, we met Jesse and he was brilliant so I felt at ease, as if there was someone on my team straight away. And that proved to be the case as whenever I had a problem at Harrow, I'd immediately go to see Jesse and he'd help me out. It was also a good time for me to remember that at Millfield, everyone kept calling me 'Mako's brother' whereas generally speaking I much prefer Billy as a name – and that's how I was known at Harrow.

I was definitely nervous when I first turned up there for real though. I had to go to a pre-season school rugby training camp which was so scary. I did not know a soul. Apart from Jesse, obviously. But none of the boys. The hardest part was they'd all been at the school for at least five years and knew the ropes and each other, whereas I was just being thrown in at the deep end for the final two years. Also the fact that many kids there came from obscenely wealthy families which mine was certainly not. That was apparent straight away.

For starters, they all dressed well. They wore quality clothes that fitted them properly, and they had more than one of everything. This was revolutionary to me. I had nice clothes but I didn't have anything that was cool, or bang on trend. My mum and dad used to give me pocket money but I always felt a bit guilty about spending it, and I would never have gone out and bought clothes. Their wardrobes were on a different planet to mine, which consisted of one pair of jeans that actually fitted me, some t-shirts and some basketball shoes. I didn't even have a regular pair of shoes that fitted my feet. And here I was at pre-season rugby camp at Harrow School, whose alumni included Winston Churchill. It was crazy. What's even crazier is how humbling it is to think about where I'm up to now, doing OK for myself in the world and comparing that to where I've come from.

At that time, I looked at those kids at Harrow and I was so envious of them. They had everything I wanted. I wished my family had been rich like so many of those boys' families. And they all seemed so down to earth, so balanced and so genuine. There's no reason they shouldn't have been that way, but it was a surprise to me. But the biggest surprise of all was that while I was initially jealous of these kids' lives, *they* all wanted something which *I* was lucky enough to have: the ability to play a bit of rugby.

They absolutely loved the sport and, for all their wealth and material possessions, all they really wanted was to be great at playing rugby. During those first sessions, we did a few drills and straight away they were asking me questions about how I did stuff. And the answer was, 'I don't know. I just grew up with a rugby ball.'

So many of those basic rugby skills came naturally to me. Once I'd stopped thinking about how privileged these boys were and how awesome it must have been to be so rich, I started to appreciate how fortunate I was.

The scariest thing about Harrow was the fact that I was suddenly living there. After spending all those years with my family, I was now going to school and when the day ended, I'd stick around there to hang out and then sleep. On the plus side, there was no going home to run with my dad, but on the down side I felt like a bit of an alien at first in a completely unfamiliar environment. Everyone seemed to know everyone else, whereas I didn't know anyone. I had to fall into the Harrow way of doing things very quickly; there was no time for the way I did things. Sleeping in? That was never going to happen. We had to be up at a certain time every morning without fail. To be fair, that wasn't especially different from my house, but I had to do it in a strange place rather than in my family home.

Then there was the school uniform. That was something else. Admittedly, I was used to wearing traditional dress for school after my experiences in Tonga, but the Harrow outfit was so English, it might as well have sat down to its own afternoon tea every day.

We used to wear a really heavy, blue suede jacket – I definitely didn't need any extra weight on me – which was known as a bluer. I then had the smart trousers, shirts and shoes to go with the bluer, but the whole look was topped off by a quintessentially English straw hat. Which would have been fine if there was one that fitted my big Tongan head. The last thing I wanted was to cause any kind of problems when I started at school, but I had no choice because they had to order a specially made straw hat for me.

That hat had to stay on at all times, even if we went out of the school on to the high street, so the whole of Harrow would know you went to the poshest school in town.

That was the weekday style – Saturdays and Sundays were different. Saturdays because we actually had to go to school at the weekend which was a major shock to me. And attending chapel on Sundays was compulsory – again, there was nothing new for me about going to church on Sundays but going to pray dressed in tails was like nothing I'd ever done before. We were also required to go to chapel on a Thursday, but I always slept in for that one as otherwise I would never have had a lie-in. And I got away with it thanks to my laid-back housemaster who also happened to be a Wasps fan.

So it all took a great deal of getting used to, but it's always like that at the start of anything. Once I'd got over those initial nerves and accustomed to the Harrow ways – and Jesse was brilliant in helping me to settle in – I soon got into the swing of it, and I became friendly with a couple of guys at the school, including Scott Spurling who would go on to become a Saracens team-mate of mine.

But the hardest part about Harrow for me was the balancing act of school life and A-level study, with signing a contract for Wasps at the age of sixteen. That meant going to training after school on Tuesdays and Thursdays and, eventually in my final year, playing professional first-team rugby at the weekend.

I've got little cousins in that school now who train with Wasps and get driven there twice a week. They have no idea how lucky they are. I used to have to roll around town by myself, getting the bus from the hill next to the school to South Harrow station which wasn't the nicest place to hang out. From there, I'd get the train to Ealing Common, clock the Nando's near the station and make a mental note to return there for supper, and then continue walking to Twyford Avenue in Acton which is where Wasps trained. By the time I got there, I needed a lie down, not a sprinting or weights session.

But I loved being part of this professional set-up and it only increased the hunger inside me to get through school and start playing rugby. It was all I wanted to do. And that was despite the modest surroundings in which Wasps used to train. It wasn't palatial, but it was absolutely perfect for what we needed and was a good lesson in showing me that for a team to be successful was far more about the people and their attitude than about state-of-the-art facilities and all that kind of thing.

When I'd finished my training, it would be time to trek back to Harrow, repeating that same journey backwards. Once I started playing more pro games for Wasps during my second year at Harrow, I had to go into training more often which made life harder as I was also studying for my A-levels and left me with very little time to get anything done. It also meant I wasn't left with much money for travel expenses, so I would usually borrow one of the younger boys' Oyster travel cards, meaning I would save on the cost of the round trip. I was eighteen at the time and those cards were for under-sixteens. If you bear in mind that even when I was fourteen I looked like a nineteen or twenty-year-old, then it was unsurprising that by the time I was eighteen, someone who worked on the tube didn't think I looked like I was under sixteen. This guy would not let me through the gate and kept asking me why I was using the wrong Oyster card. 'Mate, I don't have any money and it's the cheapest way to go,' I pleaded. Fortunately, he let me go through which was so nice of him, and that was the last time I borrowed a child's Oyster card.

Whenever those training sessions finished though, I was absolutely ravenous and no amount of protein shakes or any other energy drinks was going to cut it. With Nando's next to Ealing Common station, it wasn't difficult for me to undo any of the good work I might have just done at Twyford Avenue. I always ordered the whole chicken and chips, and would usually have half the chicken that evening, and then demolish the rest of it the following morning.

Sometimes, if I felt I could wait until I got back to school, I would order pizza in. Because I'd missed the school evening meal due to my training, I would ask my housemaster for special permission to order food. On Tuesdays, that would mean the Domino's Two For Tuesdays deal which, as you'd imagine, meant I would have two pizzas for the price of one. I'd have the large barbecue-based meat feast with extra garlic and herb sauce pods, just in case the pizzas weren't unhealthy enough. Once again, I'd have one for dinner and then smash the other one for breakfast the next morning. Sweet.

But probably not so sweet for my strength and conditioning coach at Wasps, Ian Taplin, another great guy who helped me develop at a crucial stage of my early career. Taps took me under his wing as soon as I arrived at Wasps and we got on really well, and he'd even come to see me at Harrow and do a bit of work with me there too. His main goal was to get me into better shape and harness my strengths. Behind all that, was a long-term target of trying to get me to shed a load of my excess weight. Which was easier said than done when I was wolfing down Two For Tuesdays with abandon.

But Taps was shrewd because he never made it obvious that he was that bothered about my weight, which took the pressure right off me. It also meant that I continued with my bad diet, but at that stage my weight wasn't the priority. So when he weighed me at training, he wouldn't let me see the scales. He'd say, 'I don't want you to worry about it. I'm not worried about your weight, I'm worried about all the things around it, like the rugby and all that.' His plan was based around the restrictions he knew he was working with, as I was at school at Harrow and it was impossible for him to control my nutrition as we had set meal times and set menus. His plan had to be based around the restrictions of me consuming loads of Domino's and Nando's and drinking Red Bull by the bucket-load. I'd drink it like water, as I just had no idea how much sugar there was in those cans. So while my fitness and strength did improve, by the time I left Harrow my weight had ballooned from 124kg to 152kg (not that I knew the numbers at that time) which eventually lead to that diet that ended with me in hospital.

Taps focused on my strengths instead of my obvious weakness. He knew that I would've already heard the same things from plenty of people. The usual comments, like I was too fat, too heavy and too unfit, which were not necessarily all accurate. Instead, he acknowledged the fact I was a bit of a physical freak – his words, not mine – so we focused on getting me stronger and faster because he knew I'd get fitter as we went along anyway. Assuming, that is, I would actually make it to the gym.

● ● ●

'That's it, Billy,' says the physio. 'All done.'

'Thanks mate, that was great,' I reply.

It's a Tuesday. I've done a day at school and I'm in Acton with Wasps now, but I'm feeling tired. It's hard going to school then going to training. This is why I used to hate doing running with my dad after school. Actually, I hate doing running whenever or wherever it is. But especially when I'm tired.

This training with Wasps is cool. I always start here in the physio room, then it's weights, then maybe some sprints or something. But I've had my physio and I'm not that keen on moving to the weights room yet.

If I hang around in here for a bit just chilling with the guys, maybe I won't have to lift as much. Maybe I won't have to lift at all.

So I sit on a chair and just chew the fat for a bit.

'Been a good day so far?'

'Yeah, Bill. Very busy, as usual.'

'Lot of injuries at the moment?'

'So many, mate. Doing overtime in here on the boys.'

'Nightmare.'

'Part of the job. How's school anyway?'

'Sweet.'

'Working hard?'

'Yeah, a bit. It's tiring doing school work and rugby training though. Hard to fit everything in.'

'I bet.'

'I just wanna play rugby to be honest.'

'You've got to get your A-levels though, Bill. You never know.'

'Yeah, I know. Wish I didn't have to though. It's so boring.'

Someone else is on the treatment table now. I'm still sitting here, and the clock has been ticking. I might miss weights. The physio doesn't seem to care. If he's not telling me to get on with it, then I'm not going to volunteer myself.

But it won't be long before my trainer Ian Taplin is in here. He knows me too well. But if he wants me, he's going to have to come and get me. Show me how much you love me, Taps!

But there's no sign of him.

I'm so tired that I decide to lie down on one of the physio beds. I'll just rest up here for a bit until it's time for weights. Resting is very important anyway, so this is probably better for me right now than actually doing anything too physical.

We carry on chatting. I'm feeling pretty relaxed.

Someone comes into the room. It's Taps.

Oh crap.

He looks at me. He looks at my horizontal position on the bed. There's not a flicker of a smile on his face as he says, 'What are you doing?'

'Ah, I didn't know what we were doing,' I say.

This is not true. I know it's not true, but as I sit up on the bed I have to say something.

He's still staring at me. His face is deadpan.

'Er, are we doing weights?' I say, as innocently as possible and I think I've absolutely nailed it because he's almost smiling. Almost.

'Yes, of course we are, and of course you know that.'

Didn't quite nail it, did I?

I'm up off the bed now, resigned to my fate but I'm not exactly bouncing out of the physio room and down the corridor to the weights room. I'm moving fairly slowly to show my complete lack of enthusiasm for what I have to do.

As I leave the room, Taps stands behind me, places both hands on my back and starts shoving me forwards.

'Let's go, Billy! Weights time.'

I'm smiling now. I don't turn around, but I'm sure Taps is smiling.

It must make a funny sight for anyone watching. Taps is a small, skinny guy and I'm . . . well, I'm a huge Tongan bloke. Yet, the tiny guy is shoving this massive bloke down the corridor, straight into the weights room. And the giant Tongan can do nothing about it.

● ● ●

I'm doing upper body. I'm lifting. I'm lifting so much. It's hard work. I can do it. But this is really hard work.

My biceps are straining.

My shoulders are aching.

I'm starting to sweat.

This is the penultimate set, so I'm nearly done. I need to focus on that. Maybe Taps will let me off the last set? Maybe I can get away with it?

I stop lifting and look straight at him.

'Do I really have to do another set?' I wince a bit to try to show him the stress my body is under and the pain I feel.

Taps is completely unmoved.

'Yeah, we do,' he says.

And so we do. Well, I do. I get through it, gritting my teeth and focusing on each repetition, one by one.

I drink some water and breathe. I keep breathing, recovering, preparing for what's next.

And what's next is something straight out of a Rocky training montage as Taps and another coach sit on a little sled, which I have to then pull along the floor.

I feel like I have to use every muscle in my body to do this, including some that I didn't even realise I had. If 'Eye of the Tiger' was playing right now, I swear they could put this moment in the next Rocky film. Have some of this, Sly Stallone!

I'm totally finished when this is over. I can barely move. In the back of my mind, I'm thinking one of my dad's brutal running sessions might be preferable to this. But I know that's not true. Because somehow this is fun. Because this is real and I love it.

● ● ●

Training at Wasps with Taps was actually fun. I think he understood that there was more chance of me turning up there twice a week if he made it enjoyable. The drills we did together were endless – loads of short sprints over ten and twenty metres to try to improve my acceleration so that I would be more likely to knock over whatever was in front of me when I was carrying a ball during a game.

We also did loads of work on my agility and changes of direction. That was really important, because I was suffering with so many frequent ankle injury problems at the time that I was playing less and less. My body just didn't have the ability to cope with all 130kg of my weight going through one leg whenever I turned, so the exercises were designed to help me get stronger and reduce the risk of injury.

So the training was practical and I could see its effects in the games which I was fit enough to play in. Not only that, it set me up for the discipline required to train at a professional club for years to come. Taps was great because he was really interested in who I was and my background. I explained our whole Tongan culture, how we roll, all that kind of stuff, and he loved it. In fact, he loved it so much that when I asked him if I could bring some of my Tongan boys down there to train, he had no problem with it. Often, some of my boys would ring me up to find out what was going on, and what I was up to. I'd say I was going to training so they asked if they could come. Taps was very welcoming to them and we'd all train together which I really enjoyed. I remember laughing through those sessions way more than I remember actually doing any hard work. So that was a smart move on Taps's part. It was also part of his strategy to get me prepared for being in a professional team environment which could be very weird if you weren't used to it. By getting me to talk to him about my life and my family and open up about myself a bit, he was making sure that I would be more socially tuned in for that next step.

I used to hang out with all my Tongan boys a fair bit at Harrow too. They weren't allowed to stay over, but they'd often come just so we could chill out together. That was really important to me as well, as being at Harrow was the first time I'd really been on my own after spending a lot of time being so close with all those guys. I really missed them so welcomed their visits, plus it was always funny to see everyone else's faces when a load of young Tongan blokes wearing hoodies would stroll around the Harrow campus looking like they owned the place. Let's just say that they didn't exactly fit in.

It also took me a while to feel like I fitted in there, and just because I was involved with Wasps and England Under-18s, it didn't mean being given preferential treatment. I had to do my schoolwork like everyone else.

I was studying for three A-levels while I was there – Business Studies, Photography and PE – and there's no way you can take short cuts with any of those. Not that Harrow would've allowed that to happen anyway.

I found that out early on when I got behind on my prep – homework to you and me – and had to face the consequences. It was fairly early days for me at Harrow and I was still trying to work everything out. There was a whole load of rules and a strict regime to follow, with no excuses for not doing so. One of the rules was that if you fall behind with your school work there, then any extra-curricular stuff you might be involved in had to take a back seat no matter what. If Winston Churchill himself hadn't finished his prep, then he wouldn't have been allowed to go smoke his cigars or whatever he did in his spare time there.

Likewise, when I fell behind with my homework, I received a bit of a shock to the system when I went to speak to Jesse about joining up with England for an Under-18 training camp weekend. He was as nice about it as he could possibly be, but he explained to me that I would have to stay at Harrow and miss the first day of the training camp because I hadn't done my homework. Not only that, but I would have to do a shift in the laundry room as a punishment.

That was certainly an eye opener to me. If I didn't do homework back home, I might have ended up doing extra training with my dad, not missing it altogether. Instead, Jesse called John Fletcher, the England Under-18s coach, and had to tell him I would miss the first day, and he agreed that it was something I had to learn from so didn't push back at all.

So, while everyone else in my year disappeared for a long weekend off school, one Friday morning when I should have been reuniting with my

England colleagues, I was folding everyone else's underpants and shirts in the laundry room.

Now obviously that's not the kind of thing I would want to do out of choice, but I did have a laugh that morning with my new laundry mates. I know it was a punishment, but I was always going to try to make the most of it. It must have looked pretty funny from the outside. There was a line of us all sorting and folding the washing, made up of about six or seven little ladies and a giant Tongan guy stood right in the middle of them. But we all got on well, and we were chatting away with plenty of banter flying about and I really got to know a few of them. After that, whenever I saw any of the laundry staff around the school, I'd always say hello to them and have a chat while my school friends would look on with puzzled faces which suggested they were thinking, 'What the hell is he talking to them for?'

Once I'd sorted out all the dirty laundry and folded the clean washing and put it in the relevant house boxes, I then had to help deliver it to all the right places. I did this with an Irish lad who seemed to know every-thing there was to know about the horses and gave me a whole load of tips, but that's just not my thing so it made no sense to me.

My laundry shift must have gone fairly well as my new colleagues all asked me to come back another time, but I gave them a polite smile and said, 'No way!'

It worked out pretty well for me actually. Not only did I enjoy my pun-ishment, but after getting the train up to the England camp later that day, I found out that I had also missed a massive fitness session that all the England boys did that morning.

I was injured for a fair bit of my time at Harrow so I wasn't able to play as much rugby as I would have liked there, but the weekends when I did play were great because it meant the family would come and watch and then we'd all hang out. And when I say the family, I mean probably most of the Tongan community in the UK. It was always great to see my uncles, aunts and cousins as well as my parents and sisters, as I missed that whole scene while I was boarding. Growing up around all these people meant I was really used to a busy house with people popping in and out. When it was suddenly gone, I really appreciated all those moments when we could be together.

The rugby was fun too, and I'll never forget going to play in the 2010 Surrey Sevens tournament, when we took a team full of forwards to compete with the best schools in the country. It's not really the done thing but all the Harrow backs had to play football, so we had no choice. We probably had the biggest but slowest ever sevens squad in the history of schoolboy rugby.

You'd see the other schools turning up like pros with their support staff, masseuses, and tactics boards. We just boshed a few Lucozade energy gels down us and didn't really think about winning or losing. We went out there and had fun, with me and Scott Spurling running everywhere and doing ridiculous things like smashing in drop goals from the corners.

We rode our luck all the way to the semi-final where we finally ran out of steam against Millfield, who had a plan and passed the ball around. We just couldn't catch them, but it didn't matter too much.

For me, that was one of the last times that I would be on a rugby pitch where it felt like I was having fun and the result didn't really matter too much. I had a smile on my face for most of that tournament, as I almost felt a bit embarrassed about how well we were doing.

The amazing thing was how quickly things then became serious for me as, from my Wasps debut onwards, I was suddenly balancing a professional rugby career with being a schoolboy.

I remember returning from Abu Dhabi and having absolutely no interest in my schoolwork. In my mind, all I wanted to do was play rugby and not go anywhere near school. Studying for my A-levels was the last thing I wanted to do. I had an assignment due when I got back from the Middle East and I remember dropping it into school and then heading back home to High Wycombe as my cousins were all there and I just wanted to be with them.

I played another LV= Cup game for Wasps and then a Premiership game against Leeds and a big one against Bath at Twickenham in which we got another drubbing.

I couldn't believe I was playing against some of the biggest names in the game, for the same club that Lawrence Dallaglio played for. He was a hell of a number eight, and someone who created the kind of legacy at the club that I would've loved to emulate. It was a crazy situation for so many reasons and it was hard for me to understand what the hell was going on.

My plan had always been to get through school and then become a pro rugby player. But then suddenly I was playing first team pro rugby while I was still at school and completely unable to live the pro lifestyle. On the morning after a game, all my team-mates would be in for a lengthy rehab session to get their bodies ready for training and the next bruising encounter. They were doing that and there was me, sat in double Business Studies at school, wondering how I was going to play the following match when my body was in pieces.

The problem for Wasps was the club was not doing well on the pitch and they were slipping down the league. So I was thrown straight into the intense heat of that battle at the age of eighteen with the minimum of preparation, physically and psychologically. Not just that, but I'd actually missed most of the Harrow rugby season through injury, so as soon as I was fit, I didn't return to the school team, I was instead thrust into the professional game.

And then there was school. While Harrow were really supportive of me, there was no way they were going to allow my studies to slip. That place is an academic hothouse, but Jesse was very helpful in making sure I stayed on track with my studies however reluctant I was to see it all through. No matter how much time I tried to spend in the school medical centre because of various rugby injuries I'd picked up at the weekend – none of which would've made it on to my dad's ridiculously harsh injury radar – Jesse was always on hand to coax me out of there and back into my lessons. I could never have got through those times without him, and I still pop into the school to visit him for lunch every now and then.

Despite the craziness of suddenly playing for Wasps, I never felt the pressure particularly. I'm not saying I treated it like a school sevens game and tried to score drop goals from the corners, but at the same time I just went with it and did my best, knowing that there wasn't that much expected of me as I was just a kid. I just tried to enjoy the experience once I'd got over the nerves and excitement of playing at senior level. Not that they ever went away, but it was more a case of managing them and throwing myself into games, not thinking about it too much. I often think that if I'd been a bit more focused, thoughtful and considered about that time, I might have made a far bigger impression in those fledgling moments of my career. But it was an amazing learning opportunity for me as it taught me so much about how you have to focus to really get the most out of yourself. The next couple of years with Wasps were tough with injuries, retirements and relegation scraps, but those first few months while I was still at school definitely gave me a whole heap of mental toughness to deal with all the stuff that followed.

Back at school, given the juggling act I had to perform for those few months, I was quite pleased to come away with three decent A-level grades (ACC) before I left Harrow. If I hadn't been playing for Wasps by then, I'm sure I would've done better but I can't really complain too much. I couldn't leave Harrow before I'd done the same thing I did at the Castle School, and I don't mean shooting a gun at a teacher. I mean performing on stage for the whole school.

Harrow have a famous singing competition called Glees and 12s, in which twelve boys from each house perform a song in front of the whole school. It's an inter-house competition so you're representing your own house – it was probably as nerve-wracking as making my debut for Wasps. Probably.

I don't think many people at Harrow realised I could sing. They proba-bly just saw me as this big lad who played rugby. They weren't wrong about that, but I was actually a big lad who played rugby who could also sing because I'd had loads of practice at my mum's church over the years.

It must have helped me develop a bit of a voice. When the guys heard me sing they immediately said, 'Oh, you've got a good voice, come and audition.' I didn't think about it for too long and I went along and got into the twelve. We performed Queen's 'Don't Stop Me Now' and I think it went OK – at least we didn't get jeered or have any rotting fruit thrown at us.

I actually sing a lot, without even realising it. I'll always sing along to any song I know, and lots of blokes say things to me like 'only girls listen to the lyrics' and I always agree with them, 'Yeah, I know' but inside I'm really thinking, 'Bloody hell, I always listen to the lyrics and I love singing along as well.' That's just me.

And that was just me at the Castle School too, when we had a leaving party and we all performed sketches and songs. A few of us did S Club 7's 'Reach for the Stars' – another banger for my live performance collection if I may say so – and I really went for it, even knocking out a solo in the middle, because I was feeling so emotional and happy.

I didn't know it at the time – how could I ever have imagined it at that stage – but after the Harrow Glees and 12s, my next live performance would be straight after my England debut in Argentina, in front of all my new team-mates. But that was all to come.

9

Losing My Religion

Why have you let me down so much? Especially after everything I've done
for you over the years.

I've always been faithful. I've never turned my back on you. Not once.
I'm there week in, week out, as devoted as anyone could be.

Yet now, when I need you most, where are you? Come on, where are you?

Everything's going wrong. I keep losing, it's just setback after setback. I
don't even feel like I'm the same person when I'm playing. I can't do the
things that I used to do. Why have you taken away my strength and ability?
Why are you doing this to me?

I just don't understand what's going on. I don't get it. I don't get anything
anymore.

Be true to yourself, you said. And I've been so true.

Be honest to yourself, you said. And I've been so honest.

Always stay humble, you said. I don't think I could've been any more humble. I'm humble to the point where it's actually annoying me, because I'd like to not be that humble for a little while. I'd like to scream and shout from the rooftops for a bit, because sometimes that's just who I am.

But with everything that's been going on lately, I'm starting to wonder who I really am and where I'm going.

I just don't understand where you are. Where are you when I need you? This is the first time I've really needed you, and yet you're nowhere.

● ● ●

I look around the room in which I'm thinking these terrible thoughts. This horrible and endless stream of self-doubt and loathing. I'm sitting on the same sofa, staring out of the same windows with the same view of gardens, trees and houses. The same FIFA game is on in the background on the same wall-mounted telly.

This is definitely my house. Yet it doesn't feel like my house. It feels miserable. It feels alien. It feels how I feel at the moment. That everything is just not right with the world and I just can't work out why.

I'm thinking about why. I can't stop thinking about why everything has gone wrong. In the front of my mind is this week's disaster, but that's only the freshest layer on a pile of rubbish, full of freaking nightmares.

Right now, I've been dropped from the England team for this weekend's game against Samoa. But that's not what I'm even angry about. I deserve to have been dropped as my recent performances have been so poor, so I can't be angry about that. It's the fact that I can't work out why I'm playing so badly. I'm picturing myself playing in those games and it hurts me. It's *actually painful for me to think about how awful I played in those games. But worst of all is that I have no answers. I tried to play how I wanted to and how I knew I could play. The same way I've always played. All energy, aggression and action. But it just wasn't there. My body didn't feel able to do what I wanted it to. My legs felt so heavy, they had no interest in moving. I watched my performance back and saw myself jogging around when I should have been sprinting, and realised it was the best I could do.*

But, my God, what have you done to me that I can't even sprint? Why would you humiliate me like that while I was playing for my country in front of millions of people on TV? It makes no sense. I still don't get it. And I am consumed by it, totally consumed by it. It's the failure, I can't deal with the failure. I'm the child who still can't accept defeat, whether that's with England, getting trounced three times in New Zealand, or with Saracens losing in two finals, one after the other. And all that after struggling through a relegation scrap with Wasps. Is this what all the hard work was for? Is this really why I ran while I was crying my eyes out all those years ago?

This can't be part of the plan for me. Please God, you have to help me here. I pray all the time, for me, for the team, and you're not hearing me. I come to church, I do everything I can – you've got to meet me in the middle. This is not fair. I don't deserve this.

● ● ●

I can hear someone coming into the living room. I look up and see my brother. He looks back at me with disapproval. He knows the score. He knows how unhappy I am. He knows I'm not feeling the love.

195

I tell him all that again but he's already heard it and he's shaking his head all the time that I'm talking to him.

'Mate, stop complaining all the time, stop moaning,' he says with an air of irritability.

What?

What did he just say?

He's not on my side either. I thought he was, but he clearly isn't. So now I can chalk off God, and Mako, my own brother.

His words are still ringing in my ears and I try to digest them. I am moaning a lot. Could this guy actually be right? Maybe it's me and my attitude all along. Maybe that's the biggest problem here. If I could think a bit straighter about all this, I'd know. But it's all so confusing.

I'm still on the sofa as all these thoughts pop into my head, when suddenly I'm interrupted by the doorbell.

Who's that now? Mako goes to the door, I can hear him opening it and then I can hear my parents' voices. What's going on now? They never said they were coming over. Something must be wrong. Seriously wrong. I don't think I can take another setback, I really don't. Why is everything going wrong?

My parents come through to the living room and we all say hello.

'What's going on?' I ask them, praying that everything is OK and that that's a prayer which is actually answered.

My dad sits down, looks me in the eye and says, 'Look Billy, as much as we love you and as much as this is hurting, we think you're just getting too far ahead of yourself.'

I can feel myself starting to cry. The tears are in my eyes and it's not long before they're running down my face.

I can feel how quickly everything has happened to me in my rugby career to date and how my expectations have rocketed as a result. They've gone so out of control that I've been arrogant enough to question God and his role in all this.

As all these thoughts flood in, I cry more and my mum, dad and Mako are all trying to make me feel better. 'Mate, just calm down a minute,' says my dad. 'You just need to bring yourself back down to earth to being on everyone else's level, because at the moment you think you're better than everyone else.'

I'm crying even more. It's almost embarrassing how much I'm crying. But I can't help it. I can't help it because he's right. And it hurts so much. Not only that he's right. Not only that I'm wrong – and I absolutely cannot stand being wrong – but because of the fact it's slowly dawning on me that I've been such an idiot.

This has been building for so long, but I've just not addressed it or even acknowledged there was a problem.

I look at my mum, dad and Mako and suddenly the irony hits me that actually I am incredibly blessed. Where was my faith? Where was my strength? Where was the love? Where were the answers to all my prayers?

I suddenly realise that they were right in front of me all along.

● ● ●

I'll never forget that Wednesday night for as long as I live. Something so profound happened to me, that I really do believe it changed the destiny of my life, and by association my rugby career, forever. For the first time in my life, I had lost my faith. Over a steady period of time, something that was so intrinsically linked to everything I had been brought up on had gone, slowly eroded by a period of frustrating results and form on the rugby pitch. Suddenly, I was finding myself questioning where I had never questioned before. Worse, I was prepared to directly blame God for everything that was going wrong for me. I had no other answers, so this was the most convenient one. But it never felt right. When you've been raised with something that's such a part of you, it's so weird when you suddenly start to have doubts. It's as if the bricks and mortar of your whole upbringing start crumbling before your very eyes.

I'm ashamed to admit that I lost my faith during that tough year of 2014. The seeds of it were sown in the previous two years when I had been part of a Wasps team that were at the wrong end of the Premiership and were going through a transitional period with financial problems too. My confidence was damaged and it put doubts in my head. I was still able to acquit myself perfectly well, but there was less sense of achievement because of that whole situation. Then, during my first year at Saracens, we enjoyed a hugely successful season reaching both the Premiership and European Cup finals. Unfortunately, we managed to lose them both in contrasting circumstances. We were well beaten by Toulon, but agonisingly lost in extra time of the final to Northampton which hurt so much.

I tried to take it on the chin, knowing that I was off on tour to New Zealand with England in the summer. Unfortunately, that ended in a 3–0 series whitewash. I started the final game, and was sin-binned for an alleged high tackle on Aaron Cruden, which just about summed up how things were going for me at the time. After that tour, I just became like the baby who had thrown his toys out of the pram. I didn't want to know about anything or anyone, I was just in a big sulk and felt my whole predicament was God's fault and that I deserved far better treatment.

I could only think about how hard I'd worked to get to play rugby at such a high level – all that running and all those sacrifices I had to make, but mainly the frigging running – and therefore I must have deserved more than I was getting. And I'd done all this via Tonga, unlike anyone else. It was a very narrow way of looking at things which conveniently forgot all the hurdles everyone else would've had to overcome to make it too. Someone had to win and someone had to lose – but I wasn't interested in hearing any of that. I was only concerned with how I'd somehow been wronged.

I brought all that negativity into the new season with me and, while I was playing OK for Sarries, when it came to the Autumn internationals for England, I stunk the place out. I'd had a really bad head injury playing at Munster a couple of weeks before which probably didn't help my frame of mind (literally), but I just wanted to carry on playing which was probably a bad idea. So it was on the biggest stage for England where I really couldn't perform, and I think that was significant because it made me pipe down and realise the world didn't revolve around me and my happiness. Getting dropped for the Samoa game meant I could finally get to the stage where I was so distraught that my family came to my rescue and made me see where I'd gone wrong.

What my dad said to me about getting ahead of myself was so true. I only had to look straight in front of me at Mako who had to go through years and years of trying to get into the Saracens team before finally breaking through. I just turned up there and was selected straight away and I'd always been so lucky like that throughout my career. But this was the first time I suddenly had to fight for it – I wasn't used to that and didn't know how to handle it.

Another thing that changed after that night was the way I prayed. I used to pray to God specifically to win games – 'Please help us win this match . . .' – but I was only actually praying because I wanted something out of it. It was selfish of me. I was going to church because I wanted a blessing, not because I wanted to hear what the priest was saying and not because I wanted to feel the love. That was all wrong.

Ever since that day, if I don't feel like reading the bible I don't read it because there's no point in doing something you don't want to do. And you need to do things for the right reasons, not because you feel you should.

Sometimes I'll just be looking out of my windows from the sofa and I'll remember that day. Suddenly, I'll see what I actually have, how lucky I am to have my house and really appreciate everything I have in life. I've also learned to moan less and see the good even in the bad times. When I was injured in 2016 and had to miss three months of the season, my reaction was to look for the silver linings in that cloud. So instead of sulking about everything I was missing I thought, 'Oh sweet, I'll get time to go see my cousins, spend time with the boys, go see my mum and dad, and just do stuff that I wouldn't be able to do if I wasn't injured.'

My loss of faith taught me that you can't always take everything at face value as things are going to happen that help to build your character. There's a passage from the bible that says something along the lines of:

God didn't promise everything to be smooth, but during the times that are tough he's promised to give you the strength to get you through it. And that's exactly how I look back at that period – now I actually pray and thank God for giving me those tough times so I could learn from them.

When I looked up at my family that Wednesday night, I realised I'd been kidding myself because I was no better than anyone else. We are all exactly the same so I stopped taking myself too seriously and it actually helped me feel closer to God.

Within a couple of years, I was winning trophies with Saracens and, without a doubt, they would never have meant as much if we hadn't come as close as we had previously. That made those victories extra special. It meant celebrating them was even better than it would've been had it all just landed in my lap. But it also meant that at the point of victory, I remembered how the defeat had felt. When we beat Racing 92 in 2016, I didn't celebrate straight away as I knew that dejected feeling of defeat that our opponents were experiencing. I remembered how I had stormed off the pitch a couple of years earlier when we lost to Toulon in the final. There's a YouTube video in which Jonny Wilkinson follows me off the pitch trying to shake my hand at the end of that game. The truth is I had no idea it was him because he was behind me. I felt someone trying to get hold of me, but I just wanted to get off that pitch as soon as possible and didn't want to shake anyone's hand, because I was feeling so sore after losing. It was petulant and childish, but I remembered that feeling when it mattered against Racing and instead of going crazy with my team-mates, I spent a few moments shaking the hands of the Racing players because I'd been there and I knew that feeling.

That's how much I had learned from that Wednesday night – but it was more like a wake-up call than a complete renaissance, because those kinds of values and religion had been such an integral part of my life from day one. These days, as you can tell, I'm very happy and proud to tell people I go to church regularly, but that wasn't always the case. When we first got to Wales, I used to get quite embarrassed to tell my friends at school that I was going to church because, let's be perfectly honest, it's not exactly a cool thing to talk about. We were all more than happy to talk about wrestling or rugby, but going to church on a Sunday morning didn't really cut it in terms of conversation or as a way to impress your mates. Conversations on Saturdays with kids in the village would often go a bit like this:

'What are you doing tomorrow, Billy?'

'Oh nothing mate, nothing really. I'm just going to chill with my family.'

'OK, do you want to hang out?'

'Oh no, no, no!'

When we arrived in Wales, everyone in the church just accepted us and took us in, no matter that we were the only black family there. But I guess that's exactly what faith is all about as everyone accepts you for who you are. We were never going to arrive there and replicate our Tongan church traditions, so we just concentrated on embracing the local traditions and trying to be like everyone else. All the Welsh people we met were really welcoming towards us and we became friends with a lot of them, and they even helped us out as we settled in to our new country. I think they could all see we were trying really hard to fit in – especially when my mum used to make us sing at the front of the church which was border-line humiliating for me.

In those days, I would almost be praying not to go to church even though I didn't really have a choice. Given we had school from Monday to Friday and rugby on Saturday morning, when it came to Sunday morning I always longed for my parents to forget about going to church, just so I could've had one morning where I didn't have to get out of bed – even then, I valued my sleep. Nowadays, I see fewer younger people in church whenever I go. I don't know if they're asleep or just not interested, but I know that I am and it doesn't bother me anymore what other people think of me. If anything, I'd hope that people realise I'm a man of faith and that means something to them. But if they don't, then so be it.

Once we moved to Bristol, going to church meant something completely different because my mum was the Methodist minister in Thornbury. She was the first Tongan to be ordained in this country which is something we're all so proud of, but it was really weird at first to go to her church. She kept looking over at us when she was speaking and we then had to avert our eyes to the ceiling. In Tonga, you don't make eye contact with people because it's considered rude, so that's something we've really had to work on since we've been here. Every time my mum stared at us, my first thought was 'Oh no, what have I done wrong?' but then I realised that it was just a nerves thing as she was just starting out as a minister. I think her nerves were increased by her concerns that her English-speaking congregations were all listening to her speak to them in her second language. But she needn't have worried, as she was accepted and welcomed with open arms. She was always very welcoming herself and not only made time for her congregants but also for strangers who needed help. My mum and dad's kindness and example-setting doesn't end there, as they've helped to bring so many young Tongans over to the UK to try to give them better opportunities in life. I have cousins in private schools all over the country thanks to my parents – just because their sons had a talent and could earn money by playing rugby, they weren't going to sit back and be content with that. They saw that as an opportunity to help people. It's inspiring for me to see them doing that, as was their pragmatic attitude to playing rugby on Sundays.

If you remember the Toby Faletau smashed shoulder incident you'll be familiar with his dad's attitude that we were not allowed to play rugby on Sundays. The day of rest meant refraining from that kind of physical activity. But as our rugby became more serious, my parents began to understand that things worked differently in England and it was possible to be a tad more flexible. My attitude to the Sunday thing is that first of all religion is open to interpretation and we are free to find our own way. My parents made me understand that if God has given you a talent and you dedicate your life to working hard at it, then you should be able to share that talent with others and show the world what you can do. So even though Sundays are a day of rest, by sharing what we have with others, we're actually giving something back to the world on that day if we do have to play rugby. It's still strange for us to play on Sundays, but saying that, we could easily go out on Saturday night and stay out until the early hours on Sunday and not be at all worried about it.

The most important thing is that I have the support of my family with whatever I do, and they always offer me that unconditionally. When I was down in the dumps they were there for me, picking me up and guiding me in the right direction.

They are also brilliant at keeping me grounded. I honestly have no idea where I would be without their constant reminders to be humble. Probably getting in a lot of trouble for shouting my mouth off, I would imagine.

We have an extended family Facebook group and nobody on there is backwards in coming forwards. If I'd shown even an ounce of arrogance or too much pride on the pitch, you can be certain that my aunt from Australia would've been straight on Facebook telling me off, if my mum hadn't already got there first. It's stuff I need to hear though, as it keeps me level headed and teaches me so much about perception. When you can see how other people see you, it's a massive eye-opener and really helps you to understand more about yourself. 'Don't do that, it's not right. People will probably perceive it like this,' my aunt would say. Everything in my rugby career happened so quickly when I was young, so it was really useful to hear all this feedback, but I'm actually off Facebook now which is probably better for my sanity. My aunt has got my phone number if she still feels the need to tell me off.

I'm also kept on my toes by my family's ridiculously relaxed attitude about winning and achievements. It's almost funny just how ambivalent they are about success on the rugby pitch. It's never anything to shout about, you just keep your head down and get on with whatever's next. When I was growing up, I literally had no clue about Sione's successful rugby career. It just wasn't mentioned by my parents, and Sione never sat us down to tell us stories about his glorious moments on and off the pitch. It was only later on in life that I found out that he used to be captain of his country and went on to coach Tonga to their most famous ever victory over Australia in 1973. That's absolutely huge! Yet not a word was ever spoken about it. I wasn't even certain that the guy had ever played rugby for goodness sake! I assumed he must have, but that was about the extent of it. Some people would dine out on those successes for the rest of their lives and it would be hard to blame them. But my family are far more relaxed about those kinds of things. Nothing is ever a big deal for them.

I remember when Mako and I won the Grand Slam with England in Paris in 2016, there were great scenes of joy and celebration all over the pitch and in the changing room after. Guys were drinking champagne out of the Six Nations trophy and you've probably seen that YouTube video of me singing and dancing to the Backstreet Boys. We were elated, but how do you think my parents reacted to the news? 'Good job, now stay humble and we'll see you when you get back.'

It's funny, but that's totally normal to us. When Mako and I were both called up to the Lions squad to tour New Zealand – which I sadly had to miss due to a shoulder injury – I have no doubt they were proud, but their most pressing concern for 2017 was my sister Ana's 21st birthday. In a way, that whole playing it down thing does kind of help because it can take away any pressure that might be there sometimes.

My parents also practise what they preach. Being educated to degree standard is unusual in Tonga. It's definitely a big deal as Tongan people would want others to know they are smart, but my parents would never make a song or dance about it. But that doesn't mean they don't have pride for their own achievements or mine and Mako's. I know that my dad is immensely proud of what I've done so far, mainly because he was so worried about me as I was such a nightmare when I was growing up. He was always concerned about where this black sheep of the family who was always getting into trouble would end up, so it was a huge relief to him when he realised I was a good enough rugby player to make it as a professional. I think he thought I was going to end up on the scrapheap somewhere. So when he hears now that the boys have gone out for the night and I didn't drink but Mako did, and that I was looking after my brother and cousins, he is both relieved and proud at the same time.

Whatever my childhood was like, I learned so much about the importance of family and we still see each other so often no matter how busy our lives are. I'd like to see my mum more but the rugby takes up a lot of time – and I know that Tiffany and Ana are always hanging out with mum so that makes me feel better about that. And my mum knows that she can still be a mum to me when necessary.

When I was recovering from knee surgery in 2016, everyone rallied round. Even my dad, who still insisted that medical science was wrong and that the surgery was completely unnecessary, was over at my place. He may have been lying asleep on my sofa, but he could easily have slept on his own sofa so it was a touching gesture of support. My mum was trying to do everything she could to help me. She was certainly not playing this one down. One afternoon, she was sitting at my kitchen table with her iPad, and she looked up and said, 'Do you want a cup of tea?'

'No thanks.'

Then, she was back on her iPad for a while.

'Do you want a cup of tea?'

'No thanks.'

Five minutes later: 'Do you want a cup of tea?'

'No thanks.'

She went back to the iPad for a little bit.

'Do you want a cup of tea?'

'Mum! I don't want a cup of tea, OK?'

'OK, what *do* you want?'

'Nothing!'

But she just wanted to help me so much and it made me love her even more. My sisters were also here to help and there were loads of other family too, little cousins walking around with cakes. My parents treat my little cousins like their grandchildren as they obviously cannot wait to have grandkids of their own. But those kids have got them just where they want them. They'll ask for a McDonald's and two minutes later, the McDonald's will be there. When I was a kid, I'd have been waiting around six months for a treat like that.

There were that many people coming to visit me, it was as if I was playing a Saracens home game. Because they are all so supportive, a huge bunch of aunts, uncles and cousins all turn up to every home game. Quite a few of them drive over from Bristol each time which shows me how much they care. The only problem is sorting them all out with enough tickets for each match, but luckily Mako and I can share the load and take care of everyone.

So when those tough times come around, it's great to know that I am surrounded by love and support. Unfortunately, losing my faith was not the only time I needed it, because a few years before that my career had been on the line before it had even got going.

● ● ●

'Look, it's absolutely fine,' I say to the nurse. 'There is nothing wrong with my brain.'

I'm looking at the nurse, or is she a doctor? I don't even know. But I'm looking at her and telling her the truth. But she doesn't seem to be taking me seriously.

'You have to keep still throughout the process,' she says.

'It might feel a little claustrophobic in there.' she continues. 'Have you ever had a brain scan before?'

Why isn't she listening to me? She's starting to wind me up. There's nothing wrong with me, so why is she treating me like there really is something wrong with me?

She's not even a doctor, so what the hell does she know?

I'm getting really annoyed now. 'Yeah, I've had one before,' I say. 'But I don't need one because I'm fine. I'd know if there was something wrong with my brain, OK?' I think I say the OK quite fiercely, maybe a bit too fiercely for her liking as she looks at me with contempt.

'We're doing it now so please keep still,' she says as coldly as possible and that's it. I'm on my way into the machine. I suppose there are worse things that I could be doing so it's not all bad, but I'm just quite irritated by the fuss over nothing.

I've had quite a few concussions since I started playing for Wasps,

209

probably smashed into one too many people for my own good but this is rugby. It's a tough sport, my head will be fine. Won't it?

I look around and can't see much, just the chamber I'm in for my scan, surrounding me. I'm sure this is just a waste of time. My brain feels normal. There can't be anything wrong with it. There just can't. Sometimes, you just know these things and I just know.

But you can't argue with medical people. Unless you're my dad, you can't argue with them. I haven't even told my parents about this scan. The club made me do it, after all these knocks I've been getting.

I'm kind of annoyed it's been allowed to go this far. But you just can't argue so what can I do?

● ● ●

I'm sitting in the specialist's office now. It's pretty nice in here, good furniture and all that stuff.

There are two people here with me from Wasps sitting on these lovely chairs, so this must be quite serious or they wouldn't have bothered trekking over here.

The doctor's talking to us, but I can't take it all in. It's a lot of gibberish, but I'm catching stuff that he's saying and it doesn't make a whole lot of sense.

'Your brain might be slightly too big for your head,' he says.

Is this some kind of wind up?

I've been inside my body for as long as I can remember and I'm almost certain that my brain has always fitted in my head. I don't remember ever *seeing it sticking out, but maybe it did that when I wasn't looking in a mirror?*

The doc's still talking. He's talking about a line inside my head that my brain needs to stay within, but apparently it's just outside it. Any knocks to it could be a big problem now and lead to a serious injury.

Oh, right. OK. It's parked badly. Well, that can be fixed I would've thought. You're the doc after all.

The doc is saying my name now. And I'm just staring at him.

'Billy?'

'Billy?'

'Billy?'

'Yeah,' I finally mutter, because I've been busy thinking about my brain moving as I've never realised that's even possible.

'You might have to give up rugby.'

I don't say a word. I think a lot of words, but I don't actually say any. The doctor continues talking while I think about what he's just said.

If he thinks he's going to drop a bomb like that and scare me, he's so wrong. Because there is no way in hell that I've worked as hard as I have, run as far as I've run, to get to the point of turning professional, and then have it all taken away from me because of some badly-parked brain.

No way.

Not a chance.

That's not happening in a million years.

But I don't say anything to the doctor. I won't show him any weakness and I will stay strong enough to get through this nonsense. He says we have to wait two weeks for further test results which will determine something about something or other. I'm not even listening anymore.

I can tell from the looks on faces that this is serious. But somehow I also know that it isn't. There is no way that God would've given me this talent to play rugby only for me to have to retire at the age of eighteen. There's just not a chance that's part of the plan for me. I know it. But I now have to be part of all this sitting around and waiting. And all these serious faces are not helping me to play this whole thing down which is what I desperately want to do.

I'm talking to Taps now and he's trying to reassure me even though I don't need reassuring. And the act of him reassuring me when I don't need reassuring is making me think that I need reassuring – which is concerning, and also extremely confusing.

'We don't know what it is,' he says.

Correct. That's why we're waiting to find out something about something or other.

'We're not going to worry about it, let's keep working and pushing through and focus on what we've always done.' Which is all well and good, except I can't train at the moment because of all this ongoing drama.

And this is the one time where I don't just want to hang around on the physio's bed, chatting and chilling. For once, I'm actually ready and willing to go and do some hard work. But maybe that's because I know that I can't. Who knows? This is all a bit like being stuck right in the middle of a riddle. With no way out. Well, not for at least two weeks anyway.

Taps is looking at me. He knows me quite well and, if he can read me, he'll be able to see that I need a lift. Maybe just a little something to hold on to.

'Look,' he says. 'If you don't make it, I'll get you to the Olympics as a handball player. If nothing else, you'll fill the goal, won't you?'

I'm smiling. He's laughing.

It'll be OK. I know it.

● ● ●

The truth is, I did not believe I was in any danger. But everyone else did. And that obviously made me have the odd doubt here and there.

The Wasps physio Helen O'Leary was very good as she tried to keep me in shape even though I couldn't train. My biggest concern was the loss of activity during those two weeks at a time where I was working so hard to improve my general fitness. I knew I was coming straight back once we'd been given the all clear from the specialist, so it was kind of frustrating.

Sure enough, once those very long two weeks were over, we all found out that there was no cause for concern. My brain was cleared to stay put exactly where it had decided it was most comfortable, which felt to me like the exact same spot where it had always been. And I then paid for that lost fortnight, by being flogged in the gym for the next eight weeks, so I wasn't exactly overjoyed with that.

But, I suppose the fact that I was cleared to resume training and playing again was the most important thing. Even though I was so certain that everything was fine, I have to acknowledge that it was precarious and everything was hanging in the balance, just for those two weeks. It could've gone seriously pear-shaped for me at that stage. Thank God it didn't.

10

Dark Places

London, 15 October 1999

This is unbelievable. Just unbelievable.

I'm sitting in the most amazing stadium I've ever seen, with the greatest view I've ever seen. I've witnessed it on TV before, but you can't believe the size of this place until you're sitting miles up in the stands with that beautiful green pitch below you.

It's extraordinary. It's amazing. It's Twickenham.

And even though I'm not yet seven years old, I know now that I really want to play here one day. Just like my dad is doing right now – I can see him from up here. He's a tiny figure motoring across that lush green surface, proudly wearing the red of our tiny country Tonga.

High up here in the stands, my family are all sitting, watching, cheering and doing everything we can to help our dad and his team-mates. I'm so proud of him.

Yet all I can see are hordes of white-shirted men swarming all over those brave, red-shirted warriors. I imagine myself in red, charging through the white barricades, helping my country to a glorious World Cup victory.

But there's nothing glorious going on down on the pitch at the moment, because we are losing, and now I can see there is a commotion going on. Reds and whites are clashing, pushing, falling over. It looks fun. Everyone in the crowd is on their feet now, so I can't see exactly what's happening.

Eventually, they sit down and I can see my dad talking to the referee. I hope he's not in trouble. I start to feel nervous. The reds and the whites have been split apart and are all standing in their own groups together.

My dad is still talking to the referee and suddenly another player in Tongan red joins them, but he's not standing there for long because the referee has shown him a red card.

This is not good. This is really bad. He's walking off the pitch, and my dad is left to go back to the rest of his team and explain to them what has happened. I wish he would explain to me what happened.

Everything's a blur now. It's a blur of white and I can't really keep up as the English score try after try. Each score hurts me, my dad, my family and our pride.

But I'm still so proud that my dad is down there playing. One day, I have to come back here and make things right. That's all I know right now. And it's making me feel better.

Salta, 8 June 2013

What the hell is that noise? That beating is so loud, there's no way it can be my heart. But, somehow, it is my heart. I've never actually heard it out loud like this before.

And it's running so fast. It's ridiculous how fast this thing is going. I need to calm down. If I don't calm down, I'm going to pass out.

I look up at the clock and see that we're midway through the second half.

'Am I going to get on the pitch?' I think to myself, while my heart continues to bang away like it's a tune being blasted out of the speakers at some hardcore trance nightclub.

I'm wearing the crimson red shirt of my country, and I can hardly believe it. What a journey it's been to get to this point. I think back through the years of graft, and goosebumps spread down my arms and neck. My heart goes even quicker.

One day, I dreamed of pulling on the red of Tonga; now I've pulled on this England version of red, and I could be about to make my debut.

But I'm not sure if I actually want to get on. If my heart's like this now, what's going to happen when I get on to the pitch? I actually don't know if I have the bottle for this. Even though it's everything I've ever wanted, if I don't calm down I'm going to ruin the whole thing for myself.

The mega beating goes on. I'm surprised my team-mates on the bench alongside me aren't asking me to turn it down. There are fifteen minutes to go now.

Suddenly, I look up and I've got the signal. This is actually happening right now. I stand up, and I can barely get the training top off because I'm all fingers and thumbs.

I really need to calm down. But I don't know how to.

I pray to God. Please make everything go OK when I go on.

My heart is still beating like a madman. I pray to God again.

And still it goes on. I swear I'm going to pass out before I actually make my debut and that'll be it for me forever. Just calm down!

I pray to God again. Please make everything go OK, and get my heart to chill out for a bit.

I'm ready to go on, just waiting for the referee's whistle. I pray to God again. I don't know how many times I've prayed. I actually can't stop praying. And I can't stop my heart beating at this crazy speed.

I can hear the referee's whistle. This is it. It's time. My time. All that hard work, all those hidings, all of my tears. It's all for now.

I'm on the pitch and I'm playing for England. And I'm almost out of breath just from running on. I really need to calm down. I pray to God again and off we go.

All I can do is run around like a headless chicken, smashing into everything that moves and hoping it's an Argentine player rather than one of my own.

It seems to be going OK, as I get a few pats on the back from the lads.

It's a frantic ten minutes or so, and we're winning easily so there's no pressure. I'm going to be on the winning side, unlike my dad that day at Twickenham.

It's now the last action of the game and we have a scrum. We're going forward, the ball's at my feet so I scoop it up and plough ahead, with my eyes almost shut. I wipe out two guys and suddenly I'm under the posts putting the ball down for England. Scoring a try for England. Scoring a try for my country on my debut.

Everything's a blur. I'm out of breath. I feel like I've been out of breath all night. Hang on, the referee is asking to look at a replay. Don't do this to me. Not on my debut. Please don't do this. My breathing is even worse now.

But it's OK. It's still a try. It's still a try on my debut. I think I can get used to this. If I can just calm down.

●　●　●

It actually took me around fifteen or twenty England matches to feel calmer in my head and my heart, and not to have to battle those intense nerves. They just became part of the whole performance of playing international rugby as I felt my way in to that level. Eventually, I settled down as I grew in confidence and felt more certain that I belonged in that arena, lining up alongside those players, competing against the best guys in the world.

That night in Argentina, we celebrated the win back at the team hotel and I had to stand up and sing in front of the entire squad and staff. It wasn't quite the same as performing on stage at the Castle School or the Harrow Glees and 12s. But I suppose those experiences might have helped me as I stood up and surveyed the room, about to bow to the same tradition as so many England debutants before me. I was stone cold sober but I was hoping that the boys would all be getting drunk to take the pressure off me, although I could see that wasn't the case. Instead, they waited silently and patiently as I cleared my throat, took a deep breath and began belting out Tina Turner's 'Proud Mary'.

The boys were all over it, so it wasn't long before I had a choir helping me out and the whole thing became really funny. It could've gone either way, as I discovered when Marland Yarde tried to sing a Chris Brown song and got booed. 'Mate, why Chris Brown? You've got the deepest voice in the world!' was my helpful feedback to him.

As happy as I was to have made my England debut, there was also a huge sense of relief, because I had been due to play in the Six Nations earlier that year but that hadn't quite gone according to plan due to an injury jinx.

My involvement with the England senior team didn't get off to the best of starts. In fact, it almost didn't happen at all. I was on my way back from Cardiff where I'd spent the weekend with Toby and Josh Faletau. I was feeling pretty tired after a night out, so when my phone started ringing and I didn't recognise the number, I just ignored it. I didn't need anyone hassling me when I wasn't feeling 100 per cent.

The phone rang again and it was the same number. 'Nice try,' I thought, 'but I think I would've answered the first time if I was interested in taking your call.'

So I ignored it and it went quiet which was a relief until it started ringing again. I could not believe the liberty as I looked at my phone screen, except this time it was my brother. So I picked it up and took the call.

'Hello?' I mumbled.

'What are you doing?'

'I'm on the way back from Cardiff.'

'Pick your phone up, you dick! It's Rowntree!'

'Oh! Is it? Sweet, OK I'll pick it up now.'

Oops. I'd just ignored two calls from the England forwards coach Graham Rowntree. Probably not the best way to impress someone who's going to be instrumental in deciding whether or not I play for England at any point soon. But then I had absolutely no inkling that he was going to be calling me. This had come right out of the blue, so how was I supposed to know? If I had known, I probably wouldn't have had a night out with Toby and Josh so that I could've been on my best form to talk to the gaffer.

The next time Rowntree called I picked up and did my best impression of someone who wasn't on his way back across the country after a night out in Cardiff. It was good news. He was inviting me to train with the England Six Nations squad at the pre-tournament training camp in Leeds. He wanted me to provide cover for Tom Croft who was trying to fight off an injury. So no big deal dropping those calls then!

The weekend before I was due to meet up with England, I played for Wasps against Newport Gwent Dragons, Toby's team. As luck would have it, during that game I injured my ankle. Or a more accurate way of saying that would be, as bad luck would have it, Toby managed to sit on my ankle and I felt it go pop. Given what I did to his shoulder all those years before in his back garden, I probably had this one coming. But the timing of it absolutely stank.

I was having really bad problems with my ankles at the time which the Wasps medical team were trying their best to help me out with. It was a weight issue, however, and there was only one solution, but until I properly sorted out my nutrition it was going to be a recurring issue for me.

Despite the injury, I reported for England duty after that game – well, I was hardly going to miss it, was I? There were a couple of weeks of training before the Six Nations got underway, but I spent the first week doing rehab and balance work to try to get my ankle right. Because I really wanted to show I was fit just in case I was needed to play, I tried to train in week two but it still wasn't right. After a bit more rehab, I was ready to go and started training with the squad ahead of the Ireland game. With Tom Croft injured, Stuart Lancaster told me I would be on the bench at the weekend. I was buzzing. But I was buzzing too much and not thinking.

I turned up to training at Pennyhill Park without my boots. It's a fair trek back to the hotel from the training ground which I didn't particularly fancy making, so I asked James Haskell if I could borrow a pair of his boots. I strapped my ankle, laced up his boots and was ready to roll. The first drill we did was a two-on-one, where you had to run as hard as you could at your opponents. Conscious of my ankle, on my first carry I ran hard but went into the contact quite softly and just fell down.

'No!' screamed Rowntree from the side. 'Do it again!'

So I followed his instruction and this time I decided to step around my opposite number Haskell to show what I could do. A great idea in theory, but one which he read and grabbed me around my hips, swinging us both round. As we turned, my ankle got caught in the ground and, just for good measure, Hask landed on it. There were tears in my eyes as I knew that meant I wasn't going to be on the bench and it might have even meant that the whole campaign was over – all while wearing Haskell's boots and with him on top of my ankle. It was a really tough one to take, but my ankles were just a huge problem at the time.

Somehow, I got myself back fit again in the week leading up to the following game, against Italy, and I was desperate to try to make enough of an impression to get myself on the bench. The problem for me was that Tom Croft was also now fit again and was a great player who I was just providing cover for. I could feel that I wasn't getting the same kind of love in training that I had enjoyed earlier in the campaign, so I knew that my chance was gone.

After training, Rowntree, who was sitting on one of the coaching staff's quad bikes, called me over for a chat. He tried to be as sympathetic as possible, but he had to tell me that I wasn't going to be involved in the game at the weekend and there was no easy way of doing that. I was still a twenty-year-old kid and having come so close to being involved in an England Six Nations match a few weeks earlier, only for injury to have denied me, I was so frustrated. As Rowntree finished talking, I felt myself welling up. The tears started streaming down my face, and before there was time to do anything about it, I was crying my eyes out in front of the England forwards coach.

'Mate, we don't cry around here, come on!' he said, clearly completely taken aback with this huge Tongan lad blubbing like a baby right in front of him. Then, bless him, he got off the bike and gave me a hug. And I really needed one too.

At that stage, I was still so young and hot-headed. I had not found a calmer way of dealing with things. Because I'd put so much into my rugby throughout my life, I found it very hard not to see everything that happened in life or death terms. Of course it was massively important to me and it should have been as it was my career which I'd worked so hard for. But it should never have taken on that much importance that I would lose sight of the really important things in the world like my faith or my family. It all culminated in that crisis of faith I had the following year, and it was only after that November series that I began to calm down as I'd seen the light. From then on, my outlook was always ninety-five per cent positive as I recognised that you can't be positive all the time because otherwise you're not a human being. You have to allow the negative side to come through sometimes, but otherwise I try to see the brighter side of life and not get too down in the dumps about defeats or setbacks.

Since then, I've tried to take everything as it comes which I think is far more helpful for a character like me. I train and play like I'm going to work, like you do when you go to the office every day or wherever it is you go. Rugby is my job, so when I go off to the training ground or the stadium, I'm ready. I give it everything I have and hopefully it goes well both personally and for my team. Like you, I might have the odd bad day but hopefully the majority of them will be good days at work. The more I started to look at my rugby like that, the better I was on and off the pitch. I was far more rational and suddenly had the ability to make better decisions and look at everything without getting too angry. I even found time and the right frame of mind to start watching my performances again with a critical eye, accepting the moments where I might not have been at my best. Learning to be humble again really helped me to calm down and it's something I've not looked back from since. And from that point on, there have been many successes with club and country, but there has also been the odd failure too. That's only natural and I've managed to handle those better than ever before.

As I built towards becoming a better person, I simultaneously became a better rugby player. This might sound weird, but as much as I enjoyed winning the titles and the trophies, I think it becomes meaningless when the next team wins the following year. That's my attitude. It was amazing to win the Grand Slam with England in 2016, but it's all forgotten about the next time another team does it. Nobody will remember us a year or two later, unless we go out and do it again and again.

I'm very happy when I win things, but I also remember, at times like that, there are people struggling in this world. People in war-torn countries with nothing to eat, while I'm loving life because I just helped my team and fans to win something. It's possibly a harsh outlook but it's the people we share this world with, so you just have to enjoy the successes but not get too carried away. I think I started to win things because I hadn't made it my life. I took the pressure off myself and I feel like that's something that the smarter players do.

Sometimes, we might lose a game and a few of the boys will say something like 'Oh, that's ruined my weekend.' A few years ago, I would've said those exact words, but now I reply with 'Why? Let's just have a drink and we start again next week.' Because we have to acknowledge that the other team trained as hard as us to win the game, so they may well win and we may well lose. Or vice-versa. Obviously, I don't particularly like losing but you have to look at it that way otherwise you go crazy. And that's exactly how I look at the trophies I've won. I don't even know where I've put all the medals I have. Maybe I'll try to find them one day when I'm no longer playing, but as of now they're pretty irrelevant because I just want to keep moving forward and be consistent. Great people are consistent. I never wanted to be one of those one-hit wonders and I'm sure my team-mates feel the same.

That new attitude I discovered definitely helped me to cement my place in the England team. The 2016 Grand Slam was a case in point. There would've been times earlier in my career when I was awarded a Man of the Match prize after a game, and I would strut around for the next week thinking 'I'm the boy'. Inevitably, in the next match, I would be anything but the boy and would actually play like a boy – but not in a good way. In that tournament, I managed to shake that attitude after being lucky enough to win three Man of the Match prizes. Of course it was cool to get them, but my gratitude was really to my team-mates because this is a team sport, it's not just about me. And I was just happy to help the boys in any way that I could.

To be honest, the success that year was born out of exactly that kind of team spirit. Eddie Jones came in as England coach the year before and the first thing he did was try to foster much closer bonds between us, so that we would all be more sociable with one another. Like any national team set-up, there are big club rivalries and it's not helpful for players to be split into their teams when they're with their country. So he tried to build a culture where we would be there for each other, irrespective of which club we played for during the rest of the season. And that meant talking to each other much more, connecting with team-mates, that kind of thing. Most of all, we all just had a good time together both on and off the pitch which was the key to our success. I didn't have to be nervous wearing an England shirt; I could just be myself and play to my strengths. Eddie pumped me full of so much confidence that it all came out on the pitch and I felt like I never wanted to let him down. One evening, he sent me a message asking if I could go and see him before training the following day. I spent that whole night stressing about what I could have possibly done wrong, only to find out the next day that I was going to become one of England's vice-captains. It was a great honour and gave me a massive lift which must have made an impact on my performances.

For me and so many of my team-mates, when someone is boosting you and motivating you to your face, it definitely inspires you to hit new heights on the pitch, far more so than when someone is yelling right in your face, not acknowledging that you're actually doing your best.

That whole new calm outlook definitely helped me to focus more and must have had a big impact on how I performed. Taking the pressure off worked wonders, and not long after that Six Nations, Sarries won a Premiership and European Cup double – all of which I took in my stride with my new-found Zen-like philosophy. It was a fantastic time of non-Zen-like celebration and fun with not a massive amount of sleep – and the whirlwind continued, as it was then time to jet straight off to Australia with England.

I've always been someone that needs a lot of sleep at the best of times. I take naps during the days and get plenty of shut-eye at night, and I make sure I schedule my sleep very carefully. I'll keep on top of all the domestic chores so that my house is clean and tidy and all that stuff, but it's so much more important for me to sleep. If I ever feel tired, I need to sleep and nothing will stop me. There are people I know who think that sleep is a waste of time, but I think it's one of the most important things that I do. Not only does it help me recover but I always feel fresher and more 'on it' once I've had a sleep. I know you can sometimes feel tired when you wake up from an afternoon sleep, but that's only a temporary thing. It takes me two minutes to wake up properly, and then I'm back to it, but without the lingering, background tiredness.

But by the time I boarded that flight to the other side of the world, I was in the unfamiliar position of not having slept too well for a few days due to all the trophies and celebrations, so I knew I was going to crash out. The only problem with that being that it wasn't part of the England sports science team's plans for me, and the rest of the squad.

Instead, they'd devised a plan that would see us arrive on the other side of the world as fresh and un-jet lagged as possible. The idea was that they structured our flights so that we would stay awake for the first, seven-hour part of the journey and then sleep on the second leg of the trip, which was a fourteen-hour haul. We'd then arrive down under when it was morning, stay up for the whole day and then go to sleep at night, fully adjusted and tuned in to our new time zone. A well-thought out plan but not one that I could possibly stick to with my unique set of sleeping requirements; I sleep when I want and there's nothing much I, or anyone else, can do about it.

We boarded the plane for that first seven-hour leg, a flight to Dubai where we would then take a break. The instructions were quite clear from the boffins. 'Just watch movies, and try to stay awake for as much of the journey as possible. Maybe sleep for an hour if absolutely necessary, but nothing more than that, otherwise you run the risk of ruining your sleep for the next leg of the journey. Everyone got that?'

Loud and clear.

I sat down in my seat. It was business class, which was great but it was completely lost on me. I had no idea the seats turned into beds. It didn't really matter to me, because I sat down in the seat and immediately thought to myself, 'This is really comfy,' and began to drift off.

Never mind watching a movie, I don't even remember the stewardess showing us where the exit doors were. The next thing I knew I was being

woken up by an announcement saying that we were about twenty minutes away from landing in Dubai. Next to my chair was a little sleeping
pill we'd been given for the next leg of the journey. Somehow, I didn't
think I was going to need it.

The fourteen-hour leg continued in the same vein as the first leg as I
helped myself to another seven hours of sleep. Those seats are *really*
comfortable. And I still never managed to turn mine into a bed. Maybe
next time. And that sleeping pill – wherever on earth that plane is right
now, it's probably on its floor because I certainly never took it.

When we arrived in Australia, loads of the lads were struggling and
moaning because they were so exhausted from the long flight, but I
stayed up the whole day without any problem. In fact, I couldn't have
been feeling more refreshed after all that sleeping. I'm very lucky because
I have always been an awesome sleeper. I honestly think that if you sleep
whenever you want to sleep, then you don't suffer from jet lag. It's not
scientific, but that doesn't mean it doesn't work.

Equally, it probably wasn't the most scientific response to England's
troubled 2015 World Cup campaign for me to then go out partying for a
week, but it was what worked for me.

I injured my knee during the disastrous defeat to Wales and I knew I
wasn't going to be able to play in that tournament again. I'm not sure if it
would've passed my dad's very strict set of criteria for officially being
injured, but the knee ligament problem was enough to convince the
England doctors that my World Cup was over, even though we still had
two group games left to play.

Before that setback, I had at least managed to realise my six-year-old self's dream of playing in a World Cup match at Twickenham. And I even ended up on the winning side and didn't concede 100 points, which shows how much times had changed for our family.

I haven't asked him, but I'm pretty sure my dad didn't spend half a day in a gentlemen's club after Tonga exited the 1999 World Cup. But that's what I did sixteen years later, after my premature departure from the action. I got home from the England camp the day after the Wales game, and was sitting around at home with Anthony Maka and my friend Brian Tuilagi, feeling dejected.

It had been such an intense time, as the World Cup had been preceded by a tough training camp in Denver, USA with the whole squad. That itself had come off the back of a summer in which Saracens had won the Premiership and I had then spent three weeks jetting off to Australia and Tonga for a holiday, before returning to the UK in time to join up with the England squad who were heading to Denver. So there hadn't been a massive amount of time to let off any steam and, as I sat there with my cousins that afternoon, I felt like that was exactly what I really needed to do.

It was 3pm, and Maka, Brian and I decided that the best way to do that was to head to a nearby gentlemen's club. By midnight, my cousins and I decided that we'd let off enough steam and called it a night. My girlfriend Simmone was not happy but I explained to her that I was gutted about my knee and needed to clear my head. Both of which were true. Whether that meant that I had to spend the next five nights at various University of Hertfordshire Freshers' Week parties is debatable, but Simmone was an absolute heroine and let me have my space when I needed it most.

The best thing about Freshers' Week was that nobody had a clue who I was, so I could just go out, have fun and be myself. I've had a bit more exposure since then, so I still prefer to go out locally than in busy places like central London, but after that World Cup, Freshers' Week was the perfect tonic. By the end of it, I actually felt like I was going to that University. Not because I was getting so drunk that I forgot who I was – because I wasn't even drinking, as I rarely do on nights out – but because I was just able to switch off and soak up that great vibe of young people having a good time without a care in the world. It was a far cry from the intensity and pressures of the World Cup.

I was soon required at Twickenham again, however, as I was invited back there by one of the banks that sponsor rugby, Société Générale, to make an appearance at their pre-match function before the Australia v Scotland quarter-final.

● ● ●

I'm sitting down on a posh comfy chair at the front of the room.

We're just about ready to go. I don't mind these things too much, as it's a chance for me to show people who I really am. That said, I'm looking forward to watching the game once I've done my work here.

I've got a little radio microphone clipped on to my shirt, so that everyone can hear me. It's like being on TV, except this isn't going on TV.

I look to my right and smile at Ali Williams. He's a former All Black, coming to the end of his career, so we're at different stages of life, but he gets what this is all about. Let's be pros and get it done, says my smile. If a smile can actually talk. Let's hope it can, otherwise he might just think my smile is weird.

To my left is one of my England team-mates Nick Easter, who's also coming towards the end of his career. We do a bit of hello-ing and back-slapping.

At the back of the room, I can see my man Doyin talking. He's from my management company and looks after a lot of my stuff. Like this, for example. He made sure I actually turned up at this place, on time and looking respectable.

He's talking to Sofia, to whom I was just introduced a few minutes ago. She's like the host of the day, and vital to making the whole event happen. She seems nice, Doyin's been talking me up to her. Giving it the big one about how nice I am, softly spoken, a religious guy too.

And she's all like 'Oh really? Really?' And I nodded and smiled at the right times, and she seems quite impressed.

I can see him talking to her now. More nodding. More smiling. He looks in my direction, and there are more smiles and nods. Even I nod and smile back to him. 'OK, let's get on with it now,' I think, mainly because I'm not sure how much longer I can keep nodding and smiling for.

I'm feeling really tired as well. I think that week of partying might be catching up with me. This chair is really comfy. In any other circumstances, I might even consider a little bit of shut-eye but not here. Not now. Not in front of Sofia. And not in front of all these guests. I look around the room and there are a lot of people sat around tables. They all seem like a decent bunch. They're dressed very well, they look like the parents of some of the boys I used to see walking around at Harrow. It makes me feel a bit more comfortable.

Someone approaches me. I recognise him. It's Alex Payne from Sky

Sports. He presents all the rugby. We've met before. He shakes Nick's hand, my hand and Ali's too and we talk about the rugby for a bit. He says some nice stuff to me about my injury and I thank him.

He explains to me that he's going to ask us a few questions about today's game and that it shouldn't take too long. Then we all say 'OK' and 'yeah' a lot and it's time to roll.

The noise of cutlery hitting plates and murmurs of conversations die down as Alex begins introducing himself, Nick, Ali and me.

I can still see Doyin and Sofia standing at the back of the room, staring at me. They look serious. I suddenly feel completely inadequate.

'How can I be sitting here answering questions about rugby alongside people like Ali and Nick, who have achieved so much?' I think. 'I'm like an international rugby virgin compared to them. Ali has won the World Cup with the All Blacks. He's hit the highest heights of the international game, and Nick has played more than fifty times for England, including a World Cup final. And what have I done? I've played a couple of World Cup games and hurt my knee. That's about it. Why would anyone be interested in hearing about what I think?'

I try to pull myself together and get those thoughts out of my head so that I can focus on what's actually being said.

'So, it's Australia v Scotland in the quarter-final today,' says Alex. 'How do you see this one going, Ali?'

And Ali's straight into his answer as if he's been doing this all his life. What a pro. He knows the drill and when he says he can only see Australia winning, I really believe him because he's so convincing. He's got the patter, the style and the delivery down to a tee.

But, hang on a minute. I need to stick up for Scotland a bit as I actually think they can win this match.

Alex offers me the opportunity to give my views and I say that Scotland have got a great chance of winning today, and I think it should be a great game.

Nick echoes my thoughts about Scotland and a few people seem to nod in the audience. Unless they're signalling to the waiters that they want more wine, I think they might agree with me. They might agree with me and also want more wine. That's also possible.

I feel a bit more comfortable now, I'm warming to the task. Ali smiles at me. Doyin and Sofia seem relaxed at the back of the room. Yeah, this is cool. I'm getting into this now.

Hit me with another one, Alex! Come on, let's have another question. I'm up for this now.

'Billy, it's been a tough time for you since losing the Wales game then being ruled out of the tournament with injury. How have you been dealing with it?'

OK, Alex. OK.

Doyin's looking at me, all eager and ready to hear what I've got to say. I bet he can probably say the answer for me word-for-word. Sofia looks delighted her event is going so well.

'So, how have I been dealing with things this week?' I think to myself as a mischievous thought crosses my mind. The kind of thought that might, for example, make me aim and then shoot a BB gun at a teacher. Or ride a bike into a river. That kind of thought.

I clear my throat, look at Alex and say, 'Do you want the PR answer, or the honest truth?'

The room was already silent but it's somehow even more silent now.

I see Doyin start to shift around on his feet in a slightly uneasy manner. Alex turns around to everyone in the room and says, 'Let's bear in mind that everything said in here is off the record.'

I can hear a few chuckles. I can almost smell the expectancy in the air.

'As soon as I left the England camp, I was obviously in a dark place so I just wanted to go to another dark place,' I say.

'Are you trying to say a gentlemen's club?' says Alex with a grin on his face.

'Yes, that's exactly what I'm trying to say.'

The house is being brought down. There's raucous laughter echoing around the room. I'm looking at a sea of faces showing a general mixture of amusement and shock. I'm smiling.

Ali leans across from his chair and offers me his hand for a high five. I oblige with a firm slap of his palm, and Nick repeats the gesture.

Doyin is distraught. He's making signals at me. Sofia is looking at Doyin with confusion etched all over her face. She's looking at him. He's looking at me. I'm looking at them and, all around the room, everyone's looking at me.

This is fun.

'Look,' I continue as Doyin turns to Sofia and, judging by his hand gestures, appears to go into full-on apology mode. 'I'd much rather be honest about who I am and what I do, rather than come up here and talk a load of rubbish.'

Doyin is now really using his hands a lot, as if he's trying to explain something to Sofia. She, however, looks like someone who has been told a pack of lies and is far from impressed. But before I can really take this in and think about it, Alex says, 'So what did you do for the rest of the week then?'

'Oh, it was Freshers' Week so I went out to that every night,' I say, and a split second later more laughter fills the room. I'm not sure the guests were expecting this. I'm not sure if I was expecting this really. I know that Doyin and Sofia were definitely not expecting this at all.

Doyin is now frantically signalling at me. He's signalling that hard, that I think he might be waving a plane in to its airport parking space. I have no idea what he's getting at.

Sofia, meanwhile, just has the death stare on her face. Fortunately, it's not fixed on me though, it's locked firmly on Doyin, the poor guy.

The room goes quiet again and we carry on discussing the key rugby issues of the day, moving away from the gentlemen's club and Freshers' Week. It's boring but I've had my fun and so has everyone else. Everyone that is, except Doyin and Sofia.

● ● ●

Sometimes, I do stuff for no reason. Because I feel like it. Sometimes I do stuff for no reason because I just feel like it and will then stand my ground, whatever's being thrown at me as a result of my behaviour.

So when Doyin was angrily confronting me about what I'd said, I stayed pretty remorseless.

'What were you doing?' he asked me.

'Mate, shut up. I didn't know I came here with my dad!'

Not my most diplomatic response but there was some method to what he would've perceived as my madness.

The truth is I just wanted these people, the ones who are actually rugby fans, to know that I'm real. I wanted them to know that I'm an ordinary guy, just like them, who does exactly the same things that they do. It just so happens that I'm also a rugby player but apart from that, I'm no different to them.

The last thing they would want to hear from me is a load of old nonsense about what a tough week it had been and how I'd been feeling so low and had been staring at the four walls of my house day and night since the previous weekend. They wanted to know what I had actually been doing so I told them. Because, to me, that's really important. It's crucial for me to know that they understand who I really am. That behind the rugby player is a real human being who's just like them. Because I am!

I've never hidden behind anything in my life and I never will either. That's not my style.

I'm sure that the sponsors must have received plenty of good feedback from that appearance. I know that Sofia couldn't have been that angry, because I heard from her a few months later.

After England won the Grand Slam, she sent me a message congratulating me which was a very nice touch and also showed me that I'd made an impression one way or the other. I think if I'd have come out with a load of boring stuff that the fans could probably have made up themselves, then she may never have got back in touch with me. That's my version of the story anyway, and I'm sticking to it.

I also heard from Ali Williams a while later too. It was soon after I'd picked up another knee injury, leaving me sidelined for a while, and my phone beeped to tell me I had a new message. I picked it up and saw that it was from Ali. I thought it was a bit weird that he would get in touch out of the blue, and then I read his text.

'Mate, stay out of the gentlemen's clubs!'

11

Being Billy Vunipola

I look out of the window of the aeroplane. Everything is grey. Everything is wet. Is this where my dad is? Is this where he has been all this time?

'Mum, is this the UK?' I say.

'Of course it is, you idiot,' says my brother.

My mum nods. Not at my brother. At my question. She looks tired but happy. It's been a long journey.

Yesterday or the day before, it's hard to tell, we were in Longo Longo, our quiet village in Tonga where I've known everyone since I was born in 1992, nearly seven years ago. Since then, we've been to Australia and Singapore and finally we've arrived in Great Britain where my dad lives. But I don't know anyone else here.

I look outside at everyone wrapped up in coats and hats, and wonder what cold is like. I can see it, but I can't feel it. I've heard about it from my dad and others, and it's quite intriguing.

We grab all our stuff and leave the plane. We have so many bags with us; we've even brought all our cutlery and crockery. We're now making our way through Heathrow airport, my mum, brother and sisters, and all I can hear is the clinking and clanking of our knives, forks, spoons and plates. My dad doesn't have any stuff here, so we're bringing it with us. He'll be so happy.

We step outside the airport and I feel it for the first time. I'm wearing a jumper and a pair of shorts, my favourite combination, but it's not really cutting it at the moment because I now understand what cold is.

There's also smoke coming out of my open mouth which makes it open even more. Mako's also got smoke coming out of his mouth. We're staring at each other and smiling.

'This is so cool!' I say.

• • •

We're getting out of the car that we've been in for ages. I've been asleep for some of the time. I don't think I've ever been in a car for this long in my life. It's dark outside now. I don't even know if it's the same day anymore.

I stretch my arms and legs, and see that we're all standing outside a house in the dark. Suddenly, my dad appears and we're all hugging and shouting and happy.

I tell my dad about the smoke coming out of my mouth and as I say it the smoke comes out of my mouth again. He laughs at me and I hug him.

We go into the house. It's quite empty apart from a sofa. There's no upstairs but when dad tells us that, he also says it has a swimming pool.

'Where's my bedroom?' I ask, and my dad points to a room. When I go inside, there's no bed in it.

'What am I sleeping on?' My dad hands me and Mako some blankets which will be our beds for the time being.

Even though we're in the house now, I still feel like we're outside because I am so cold.

'The heating is broken,' says my dad, as if he's informing us that the curtains are broken which nobody would care about.

I'm thinking about how warm it was in Tonga when we left the other day. How did we suddenly get from that to this? Australia and Singapore were even hotter when we passed through them on the way. But this is so cold. I need to learn new words to talk about this cold. This cold is just so cold. And I'm indoors.

We put the blankets down on the floor, and stay in our clothes to go to sleep.

● ● ●

It's morning and the first thing I notice is that I'm still breathing smoke. Is that going to happen for the rest of my life? Does everyone here walk around like dragons?

I'm thinking about that while I go to have a look at the swimming pool that Dad said we have. I find it and I now understand why we won't be going swimming in this pool anytime soon because I can't see any water. I can only see ice. The pool is frozen solid. It looks the way I feel. I hate this place and I don't understand why we came here. I really want to go home right now.

● ● ●

When I think about those beginnings in this country, and then consider how I now get stopped and asked for photos with people, and have strangers yelling 'Billy!' at me, it's hard to believe the contrast.

Now, I don't have to worry about sleeping on blankets, or being cold – well, sometimes I do worry about being cold but that's just my islander roots. Now, I only have to worry about being recognised as I find it so uncomfortable. I never mean to be rude but if someone shouts my name out, I'd rather be anywhere else in the world than there at that moment. I just get really shy with any attention.

Sometimes people walk up to me and ask me, 'Are you Billy Vunipola?' and I just clam up with fear. I'm never sure how to respond. If I say, 'Yeah, I am' then, to me, that sounds really cocky. So usually I'll just quietly say something like, 'Yeah, yeah, how are you?' and just try to almost brush off the fact that I am Billy Vunipola.

That freezing cold kid in Pontypool would not believe that anyone in this huge country would have any idea who he was. But he would probably identify with all the kids who hang around after Saracens games waiting for pictures. I always do my best to keep everyone happy, but sometimes it can be a bit like hard work when I'm feeling absolutely shattered from playing a tough eighty minutes. If my parents are there, they'll notice that look on my face and will yell 'Billy! Billy!' and I know I have to fix up pretty quick and keep smiling for the pictures.

'Remember when nobody knew who you were or gave a crap about you?' they'll say afterwards.

I remember actually being like one of those kids as well. When Wasps came to play at Bristol, I was calling Josh Lewsey and Lawrence Dallaglio over for autographs and photos, so I know exactly how it feels. It seems like such a short time ago – can I really be the same kid who traipsed through Heathrow with his family's cutlery and crockery ready to start a new life? Well, I'm still wearing the same jumper and shorts combo – albeit in slightly bigger sizes – so I guess some things haven't changed. And I think those early struggles have helped keep me so grounded that without them, I might not have had the success I've had.

I didn't understand what was going on back in our early days in this country, but my dad went through times when he really struggled. It was a baptism of fire, coming from Tonga to live in Pontypool, but we all got on with it and did the best we could under the circumstances. Although I probably did my fair share of moaning about it too.

On Sione's prompting, my dad had brought all of us over to the UK, while giving up the offer of a scholarship to do a Masters at University in Sydney. Within months of us arriving he was searching for a new club and was spending every waking hour regretting his decision. He said it was the lowest point of his life and he did not know where to turn. It all unravelled for him at Pontypool, as the club were frustrated because my dad was frequently called up by Tonga to play in World Cup qualifiers – and that usually coincided with Pontypool defeats. They were playing in the second tier and failed to gain promotion and, with only eight full-time players on the books, something had to give. And that something was my dad as he had his contract cut short by a year, leaving him, and us, high and dry. He was thirty-two and he was really worried that another club would not take him on at that age. But friends and locals rallied round to help us and, much to his relief, dad managed to get a contract at Pontypridd for another year to give us some breathing space.

A year later the same thing happened as his new club decided they couldn't keep him on. Once again, he'd been taken away by Tonga, first for a pre-World cup training camp instead of doing pre-season with Pontypridd, and then by the actual tournament itself. Although he played towards the end of that season and helped his side secure a Heineken Cup slot, his time was up and when we headed back to Tonga for the summer he was determined to return home permanently.

That was the point where Sione intervened. The point where all our lives changed forever. Because even though he had no club and no work, my dad showed faith in his dad's vision and took us all back to Wales, on a wing and a whole lot of prayer, that everything would come good.

I don't know how my mum and dad did it. Somehow, they managed and Mako and I were able to thrive. When we line up for England now, it's impossible not to think back to where we came from. It keeps us humble and grounded. But then every player we play alongside or against has a story. It's not just us.

I think people who play for their clubs and country have all given up the same things. The only difference is that Mako and I have come from thousands of miles away to do it. It doesn't give us an edge over anyone else but helps us to be more focused, to think of where we came from, the time that we spent pushing towards this goal, the tough moments we've experienced and obstacles we've overcome along the way. It helps us to be more balanced and keeps us working harder.

At the top level, you can't underestimate how important that is because everyone's always striving to take your position. The competition is immense, as it should be.

I look at my cousins who are also now in the UK, trying to follow in our footsteps. That was the thing about Sione's vision. It wasn't just for us, it was for the whole family. He wanted everyone to benefit, so I now have five little cousins playing rugby in this country. The path they're taking is just a bit more well-trodden, by my own size 13.5 feet, and I notice the little differences between what I went through and what they have to do. Everything they've got so far has been easy because of me and Mako. If they want boots, they get boots. If they want kit, they get kit. If they want to sit in a hospitality box and watch Justin Bieber, they can do that. They don't know how lucky they are, and I don't think they understand what hard work is yet. I'm not saying this because I'm resentful. I'm saying it because I can see how important it was for me and Mako to have to struggle a bit when we were kids. My cousins are going to need to learn for themselves that it's not so easy.

The best thing for me and my brother was that we had to do it all ourselves. Those hard times we went through were the times where we learned the most. Those are the times that I can still lean on now when the going gets tough through loss of form or injury.

Sione assured my dad it would come good and, eventually, it did. As Mako and I started to play more seriously, my dad could see that his dad had been right to insist that we try to take the opportunity that had been given to us in our new country. Although I'm pretty sure Sione would never have imagined that Mako and I would one day wind up playing against each other as professionals. But it happened, and it was one of the toughest experiences of my life.

Before I'd committed to Wasps, I had a few meetings with Saracens as they were also interested in signing me. At the time, I think it's fair to say I had some fairly strong opinions about that club and how they went about their business. Opinions that were born out of complete ignorance, it has to be said, but views that nevertheless made for a pretty interesting meeting with club CEO Edward Griffiths, myself and my dad at a Holiday Inn hotel.

Edward was giving us the big sell about Sarries and I remember sitting there thinking that I wasn't sure if he was talking a load of crap or not. I just couldn't tell. So I thought I'd test the water.

'Mate, I don't want to play for Saracens because you guys are like the Man City of rugby,' I said, referencing how City had spent fortunes on new players and started winning trophies.

'You don't bring anyone through the Academy,' I continued, having absolutely no idea whether they did or not. That was just my perception of the club and I was going to tell him what I thought whether he liked it nor not. As it turns out, I was talking straight out of my backside, but that didn't seem to matter too much at the time.

'If you're going to say that, then we're not going to sign you,' said Edward.

'Good, because I don't want to play for you,' I replied.

As meetings about potentially signing for a club go, this probably wasn't one of my best. But at the time, I didn't care. What I cared about was that I was pretty much still a kid and some of the biggest professional clubs were trying to sign me. To me, this was an absolute revelation that showed me I was going to make it. I had become Billy Vunipola, the rugby player.

It's fair to say that I got a little carried away.

When my dad and I walked out of the hotel and into the car park, not for the first time, he wasn't happy with my performance.

'What are you doing, you idiot?' he fumed. 'You don't even know anything about them and you're giving it all that!'

But I was away with the fairies, convinced I'd already made it.

'Do you know what, Dad?' I said. 'One day, I'm going to get you a really nice car.'

'Don't worry about me, just sort yourself out first.'

My parents have never really been into material things because they always put family first, and by that I mean family here and back in Tonga. I never got my dad that car when I signed for Wasps, but I did lease one for him years later – it was something that was really important for me because I wanted to say thank you to him for everything he'd done for me.

I was always going to sign for Wasps, despite those meetings with Saracens. Even though it meant Mako and I would be playing for different teams, I liked the set-up at Wasps and the club's history as well. I had every intention of trying to create a legacy for myself there, but things didn't quite work out in that way.

The two years after I left school were probably the hardest of my career so far. On the pitch, I was thrown into a relegation battle. Perhaps if Wasps had been enjoying more success, there might not have been the need to play me as much.

But I do think I could've done more during my time there, purely because I can now see that I wasn't focused in the way that I am now. Perhaps it's unfair to criticise my teenage self as I clearly lacked maturity, but back then I think I could have tried far harder to be more diligent with training and all the extra stuff that goes with it, like nutrition. I suppose it's easy with hindsight, but at the time I would try to get the training done and then get out of there. I was more focused on going to events that we would be invited to as players. A few years ago, I would've turned up to the opening of an envelope. Anything that was going, I'd be right on it, thinking I was the man. It would usually trickle down from the top, so one of the big dogs like James Haskell would receive an invite to something he had no interest in attending. So he'd say, 'Bill, do you want to go to this?' and I would lap it up with all the enthusiasm of a hungry young puppy. Those things were more important to me than the rugby back then.

These days, I rarely do that as I try to retain my focus. I take all the fitness far more seriously as well, making sure my whole body is prepared for the physical assault it will receive from playing rugby. There's a lot of upper body work because that's the point of contact, and our game is far more attritional than in the southern hemisphere because of the weather here. I'm lucky, because as an islander, I naturally bulk up very quickly so I find that all over body work easier. When I was out with a knee injury in 2016, after a week of leg training my muscle bulk was back to its original state. When I was a kid, my biggest challenge was whether I could be as fit as everyone else and that still remains the case. That means I still have to run all the time, which also means it's still the thing I hate the most. The difference is that I'm now less likely to cry while I'm running and I'll just grit my teeth and get the job done – because I don't have a choice. Although when it came to running, I didn't really have much of a choice with my dad either. His word was final – and that also turned out to be the case when I reluctantly moved from Wasps to Saracens.

● ● ●

'I hate these guys. I actually hate them.'

My thoughts are filled with rage and anger and there's nothing I can do to stem the flow of negativity from boiling over.

'Just look at their faces, all bronzed from the pistes of Verbier and now back on the rugby pitch after their little holiday. Who do these wankers think they are?'

There's a game being played right in front of my nose, but I still can't stop thinking about how much I hate this team. With their money. And their stars. And my brother. And, next season, with me!

I don't hate him, of course. But the Wasps guys want me to hit him hard. And I can't do it. I just can't do it. It's not natural. I can smash Toby, that's different. But not Mako. He's my brother. This is so hard. And so weird.

This is not the back garden where we would tangle so often. This is the Premiership, and it's happening right now. I just can't hit him the way I would anyone else. It's not right.

We're winning this match at the moment. This is beautiful. We need to win and I need to hurt this team that my mum and dad were so desperate for me to join.

I just want to beat them too much. I know that I'm trying too hard.

I smash into someone. I don't even know who it is. One of those ski slope types who had it coming. I don't feel like I'm really focusing on the game though, I just know I have to hit people. There's a penalty and I can have a breather. I need it. I can see Mako, he's looking at me. This is so strange.

As much as we pretend we don't like each other and get on each other's nerves, deep down he's my brother and there is nothing in this world that I wouldn't do for him.

I can't really deal with this. It's too complicated.

The game has restarted and Saracens are fighting back. I'm even more wound up now, as we're losing our grip on the game. I'm tackling and hitting anyone I can. They're so close to our line, I need to stop them. I need to stop them now.

Mako has the ball. Mako has the ball. He'll score if I don't tackle him. He's about to score.

I dive on him. On my brother. It's not the biggest hit I've ever made. I kind of smother him more than anything else. But it's enough because he drops the ball. I've never seen him do that before. Did he just do that for me? For Wasps? Surely not?

There's no time to talk about it, the game is continuing. I go off in search of the ball and my next target.

● ● ●

They've turned it around. Those really irritating guys who throw money at everything – even at me – are now winning. Not content with their skiing *trip for the first half of this week, they're now beating us at the weekend. Beating me. In front of my mum. I wonder what she's thinking. I bet she's happy that Sarries are winning. I look for her in the stands, but I should be focusing on the pitch as there's a lineout being formed.*

Why do they want me to go to this club? Nobody in rugby likes them. It doesn't make sense. I want to stay at Wasps, I really want to stay. It's my club. But not for much longer.

We're losing and I hate losing. But I'm getting used to it at Wasps. And now, the coach is making changes and I'm coming off. I hate coming off. But I've not exactly been the star of the show, so I'm not that surprised.

I run off the pitch and sit down to watch the rest of the game.

I really hate those guys.

● ● ●

That game was definitely a turning point. Even though my move to Saracens had been announced, I was still confused about it. I was so keen to make an impression that day that I was trying way too hard and ended up having an absolute stinker. I was even dropped for the following week's European Challenge Cup quarter final against Leinster.

I found playing against Mako that day so hard; it made enough of an impression for me to start thinking that joining Sarries might not be such a bad idea after all.

My dad was initially happy for me to play at Wasps. He wasn't concerned about me and Mako being on opposite teams in the same way that my mum and my sisters were. Back in Tonga, he'd played against his

WRECKING BALL

brother who went to a different school and he didn't see it as a major problem. His concerns with me at Wasps were different.

He first started to push for a move after closely watching me play and seeing how Wasps were using me, even when I was still a teen. In his view, the team were very reliant on me and always used me as their first-choice ball carrier, meaning I would take a hell of a lot of hits from some of the opposition's biggest battering rams. There wasn't much choice. The squad had been unlucky with so many injuries and enforced retirements that we were at our bare bones. Although I was big myself, I was still a kid and Dad thought it was wrong. He was especially concerned as he felt my career might be over after only five years if I was to take that kind of regular punishment every time I played. And this was coming from a guy who played in some of the roughest games you'll ever see in Tonga, so if he was worried about me being pushed too hard physically then it was worth sitting up and taking notice. He's actually way more scared now when he watches Mako and I play due to the new levels of physicality in the sport and the dangers that exist as a result, which shows how much rugby has changed.

Once, after he'd watched me play for Wasps, he sat me down and said, 'Billy, you know what, I think it's better for you to join Saracens.'

'Why Dad?'

'Billy, I watched you guys play and I don't like what I see.'

'Oh Dad, I thought we were on the same side.'

'We are, Billy. Everyone wants you to join Mako at Saracens except me, because I wanted you to be happy. But being happy and being wise are two different things. You can be happy at Wasps, but you won't last long.

If you go to Saracens they have more players, better players, then you can play four games and have a game off.'

'Oh Dad, no. I don't want to move.'

We agreed that we'd hold off from making a decision, but the truth is I was just being a bit stubborn and, more than anything else, I wanted to get my own way. I was starting to see that my dad was right, but I was too obstinate to actually tell him.

The game changer for us both came after the time I was hospitalised when I became really ill due to my back and diet issues. During that episode, I was left in High Wycombe's no frills NHS hospital for most of the time, and had very few visits from any of the senior staff at Wasps.

A while later, Mako fractured his toe while playing for Saracens and was taken straight to a private hospital on the Saturday night after the game. He wasn't there for long, but the players, coaching staff and even Edward the CEO came to visit him. For my dad, it summed up the difference in where the two clubs were at that moment in time. I'm sure things would be different now with the new set-up, but back then Wasps were fighting for survival and an over-stretched management team were just trying to keep the club afloat.

Soon after, we had a chat and my dad insisted that it was better for me to leave Wasps and join Saracens. Not for the first time in my life, I cried. I didn't want to leave, but I also knew that my dad was right.

There were some great people I was leaving behind at Wasps like Taps, the physio Helen O'Leary and the kit man Malcolm Sinclair who all helped me so much. I still have so much respect for that club, for the opportunities they gave me and for everything they did for me. They taught me so much and I was able to take all that with me and kick on as a person and a player at Saracens.

My dad convinced me, but I was also very aware of how upset my mum had been at seeing Mako and I on opposing teams. It made her very uncomfortable and therefore made my decision to move far easier.

When the deal was announced, in January 2013, I received a fair amount of stick on social media. People called me out for being a traitor, and said that the club had built me up only for me to then leave, while someone else claimed that I 'should have shown loyalty because we made you who you are', all of which was not particularly nice. Or true. God and my dad had a far bigger say in making me who I am – not to mention those hill runs when I was about eight years old too. But the abuse comes with the territory and I had to tough the situation out and wear it. I also had to wear my comments to the Sarries CEO that I had made in that meeting years before, but Edward didn't take any of that to heart. He actually said he loved how much I was prepared to wind him up.

I didn't join Sarries until later that year before the new season. Once I was there, I quickly understood so much about the culture and how things work there, and I immediately realised this was a good decision – even if it was one that I felt had been made for me. Those thoughts quickly passed as Sarries welcomed me and made me understand that the club was way more about the people there than the rugby. That was something which I embraced straight away. They treat their players like kings and it felt great to be made to feel so valued. Of course, there was the bonus of now being at the same club as my brother, which was amazing considering we had shared so much of our incredible journey and would now continue to do so.

But it was more than that. Going in to train at Saracens every morning is like going into school or college to see your mates. That's how it feels. And I responded to that really well.

At Sarries, I never experience that feeling of 'I really can't be bothered today' when I turn up for training, which is something that used to happen to me a lot. With my fitness, I always used to be in great shape at the start of the year. But the long season always ground me down. The hard work got on top of me and I'd start to lose focus and let things slide a bit, coming out with stuff like, 'Oh, I don't have to do fitness today because I did it last week . . .' or 'I'll eat this treat because I just played a game . . .'

I'm not blaming Wasps for that at all. So much of the nutrition side of things was down to me – it's not like the coaches and sport science guys can follow me around all day and night, telling me what to eat and what not to eat. I just wasn't mature enough to be willing to take responsibility for my actions so I would give myself the excuses I needed to hear in order to justify anything I wanted. As a tough season wore on, I'd always find that I needed the comfort blanket of allowing myself treats and so it was easy to give myself the permission for them. Towards the end of the season I would always be feeling sluggish and everything was extremely hard work. Not only were the physical demands greater because of how tired my body was, but my body would actually be working harder to do the same things it had been doing more easily at the start of the season anyway, because I'd allowed it to get fat again. And so it went on, until I got to Saracens where I was able to get my head around it all far better. I think that was as much a maturity thing as it was to do with the club's set-up. These days, I would never say that I don't need to do fitness work. I'm not saying I love it, but I'm not trying to find excuses to get out of it anymore.

Of course, there might be the odd time when I find the prospect of going outside to do fitness drills as boring as a maths lesson. I don't particularly like doing either but I treat them the same in that I just have to get on with it, because it's going to be so beneficial to me in the long run. Sometimes, I can't believe I'm even saying or thinking this stuff. My younger self would be absolutely appalled.

It's a similar story with my nutrition, as I no longer spend time looking for an excuse to justify chomping something down that I know is bad for me. That's not to say that everything I eat is full of purity and goodness, because I obviously still enjoy the odd treat. The difference is that it happens less frequently and I don't have to come up with a story to tell myself why it was warranted. Sorry Domino's, but I know your Two for Tuesdays promotion has taken a big hit recently. I think I single handedly kept that one going for a few years . . .

I'm sure that my frighteningly mature outlook is helped by the relaxed environment at Saracens. And when I say relaxed, I don't mean that we sit around playing *FIFA* on the PS4 all day – we only do that for half a day. It's an environment that's relaxed because of the ease of the relationships between us players and the coaches. That breeds a strong work ethic when it's time to really do the tough stuff in training and start focusing. But it also means that we have a lot of fun when that's appropriate.

Team-mates joke that they always know when I've arrived in the morning, a long time before they actually see me, and that's usually because they can hear my screechy laugh. The atmosphere at the training ground means that I can just arrive there and be myself, which is usually loud, a bit stupid and just having fun. And that starts with the coaches. There will always be a bit of piss-taking but never in a completely disrespectful way. The ethos has always been that coaches and players are all in it together and I think that's really healthy and conducive to getting results.

It also creates an openness between us all, so that I feel more free to say what I like and don't like, and what does and doesn't work for me. The coaches are always receptive to that kind of feedback which really helps foster that spirit of togetherness. It's a great culture, but it's the Saracens culture that existed long before I came on board. I just embraced it and joined in.

I suppose injuries have shown me that I have to try to make the most of my career as things can change so quickly. So perhaps that also helped me focus more at Saracens, as an awareness of my mortality as a rugby player kicked in and became more real. That was never more the case than when we went to play Munster in 2014.

● ● ●

I can see myself on the big screen.

What am I doing on the big screen?

What's that loud breathing noise?

I'm in a stadium. I know this because I've just looked around and there are thousands of people here. What the hell are they doing here?

I'm looking at myself on the screen again and I'm wearing Saracens colours. When is this picture from?

I look down at myself and I've got that same kit on.

What's going on?

Where the hell am I?

Why can I only hear that breathing sound?

I can't seem to see or think straight.

Me on the screen looks up again, a second after I just looked up at me on the screen. In the background of me on the screen, is me looking at the screen.

This is so freaky.

This is like a bad dream.

Dream! That's what this is. This is a dream. No, it's a nightmare. It's one of those ones where you know you're dreaming but you kind of can't stop. But at least you know it's a dream and so it's less scary.

All I can hear is really loud breathing. I can't hear any other sounds. It's the kind of breathing you hear from yourself if you're running really fast. Or if you're being chased.

Chased. Chased. Hang on, that rings a bell. I feel like I've been chased quite a lot and maybe that's why I'm breathing so hard. But why can I still hear that breathing so loud and clear? Can somebody stop that bloody breathing? It's driving me crazy.

Someone approaches. I can see them on the big screen. I know them from Saracens. What are they doing here?

'Where are we?' I say out loud, and by saying that it kind of interrupts that crazy breathing for a second or two.

'What's wrong?' says the Saracens guy.

I can't answer him. Not because I don't know what's wrong, because there is so much wrong at the moment. But because I can't find the words right now.

Everything seems to be happening at the wrong speed. It's kind of all happening r-e-a-l-l-y s-l-o-w-l-y.

But that's because it's a dream and that's what happens in dreams. There's no time and space, so of course it feels weird like this. It's like one of those dream sequences in a movie, when time slows down and it all feels a bit trippy and mad.

I'm very confused. I have so many questions, like where am I and how did I even get here, for starters.

'What the hell's happening here, where are we?' I manage to say.

'Mate, we've just played a full game,' says the Saracens guy which totally spins me out.

We've just played rugby? Then how come I don't remember a single thing about the game? I'm only thinking this because I'm too scared to say it out loud.

Still, there's the breathing. That breathing that I can't get out of my ears.

'How did I play?' I ask the Saracens guy. If I can't remember anything, he might be able to tell me. And I need to know, just in case this isn't a dream.

'Mate, you played really well,' he says.

And I'm so relieved. I'm so relieved that I'm nearly in tears just at hearing that news.

The breathing in my ears is still loud but it's getting easier, more controlled. Less panicky.

'What's my weight?' I ask the Saracens guy and he's looking at me with a whole lot of concern.

'How heavy am I?' I say, more urgently. I need to know. I've been working so hard to stay in shape this season that I need to know if I'm OK or if I'm

too heavy. I hope they haven't put me on the screen because of my weight. I'll be so annoyed if that's the case.

But the Saracens guy won't tell me. He won't answer my question. Instead, he's putting his arm around me and we're moving slowly across the pitch together like an old married couple.

What's he doing? I only asked him what my weight was. I can see the other guys on the sidelines now.

Oh right! The Saracens guy is helping me off the pitch. The game must be over now so we're heading towards the changing rooms. I get it. As we walk, I'm starting to remember stuff. We flew here yesterday, to Ireland to play Munster. We stayed in a hotel last night. But I can't remember anything else. If my life depended on it, I couldn't tell you anything else between staying at that hotel and looking up at the big screen a few moments ago.

The breathing is still there. I think I can remember hearing it before the big screen moment. I was definitely being chased and I was definitely breathing really heavily. So I do remember some things. It's much calmer now though, I'm back in the changing room and one of the Saracens doctors is putting a machine next to me and a mask over my mouth.

What the hell's going on now?

I don't struggle, I just carrying on breathing on the doc's instructions.

'Breathe in that oxygen!' he says. And that's what I do. That's all I can do. That's all I've been doing. That noisy breathing. I'm good at that.

This is all getting too much for me now. I don't know what I'm breathing in, but it's making me feel really emotional. I can't hold it back any longer. I can feel the tears in my eyes, rolling down my cheeks. I have no idea what's going on, but I'm crying. I pull off the mask so I can sob properly.

'Why am I crying?' I say to one of the guys who's standing near me.

'Mate, don't worry. You played so well.'

I feel happy that he's said that, but it's still freaking me out because I can't remember any of this game they're claiming I just played well in. So how on earth do I know if it really even happened? Last thing I remember is being in the hotel.

I'm still sobbing and someone else tells me I did well out there.

A lot of my team-mates are streaming their way into the changing room now and they come over to me and ask me how I am.

Apart from being an emotional wreck, having no memory of a game I'm supposed to have played, seeing everything being played out in front of me in a slow-motion, dream-like state, continuously hearing my breathing so loud in my ears, having to breathe oxygen through a mask and not having any idea what my bloody weight is, I'm absolutely 100 per cent fine.

But I just say I'm fine because it's too hard to explain all that.

I've stopped crying now and I can see everything a little clearer. My world is almost being played back to me at normal speed, as I carry on breathing that beautiful oxygen. There is still a huge heaviness about everything though which I can't seem to shift. But at least I'm not crying.

Goodness me, this whole thing is so weird. I still have so many questions but the doctor tells me to keep breathing. So I do.

Keep breathing. Keep breathing. I'm not sure I have much of a choice about this.

I'm still trying to piece together all the events of the last few minutes. It's hard to get my head round it all. But this oxygen is definitely helping. Who knew oxygen could be so good for you?

The doctor comes over to check me out. He tells me I'm concussed and that I must have taken a blow to the head, but they didn't see it happen.

I tell him I don't remember anything.

He says that's normal.

But I say that I've taken the odd knock to the head during a game plenty of times before and not felt like this.

He says that's normal.

I ask him if I can stop breathing the oxygen now.

He says give it a couple of minutes and then stop but keep taking it easy.

Keep breathing. Keep breathing. It's funny, because I realise that when you try to do something that usually comes naturally, it suddenly feels really unnatural. I've almost forgotten how I normally breathe.

I think about seeing myself on the big screen. And, in my mind, I can suddenly see a seventy-eight on the screen. It was in the seventy-eighth minute that I suddenly saw myself. It was in the seventy-eighth minute that I resumed some kind of awareness of what the hell was going on – although I still don't really know what the hell was going on.

I start to wonder how long I'd been playing without having any clue what I was doing. I might have banged my head in the first few minutes of the game and been out of it since then. It kind of frightens me to think that, so I try to stop thinking it.

Keep breathing. Keep breathing.

A few more of the boys come over to talk to me. I give them the thumbs up. At least I'm not crying now. That was kind of embarrassing. But it's not the first time, and probably won't be the last.

The doctor is back and he removes the mask and reminds me to take it easy.

I sit up on the bed and shake my head. It's a kind of disbelieving shake of the head.

'Oh!' I suddenly say. 'I didn't shake anyone's hands after the game.'

I get up off the bed. I'm wearing my kit but without boots or socks. I've got no idea where they are.

I walk out of the changing room and back through the players' tunnel, bare-footed. The floor is cold. I'm feeling pretty cold too, but I've got to shake hands with the Munster guys. It's the right thing to do.

But something's not right because the stadium seems quite dark. Some of the floodlights aren't even on. I'm staring out into the semi-darkness of the stadium and there's nobody there. Did any of this even happen? Have I completely imagined this whole thing? Am I going crazy?

I'm slowly looking all the way around this huge arena, and, as I stare into the distance, the last remaining lit floodlights are switched off and the whole place is plunged into darkness.

I'm still staring. I'm still breathing. I'm standing in my bare feet in an empty, dark stadium and, once again, I have no idea what on earth is going on.

● ● ●

I've learned to laugh at some of the awful things that happened to me that day. It still absolutely cracks me up that one of the first questions I asked was about my weight. That shows just how seriously I was taking that whole side of things and how paranoid I was about staying in shape and not being too heavy.

But it's also true that the reality of what can happen on a rugby pitch is pretty frightening, as I found out in that match. I learned later that I took an accidental knee to the head from Paul O'Connell early in the second half, and that's what had caused my concussion and the resulting memory loss. Because I was so unaware of what was going on, I kept playing without saying anything to my team-mates or any of the coaching team on the side. It was only when I suddenly saw myself on the big screen right near the end of the game that I became a little more conscious of what was going on – and even then I didn't have a clue as it was all really hazy. But the Saracens medical staff were amazing and really helped me through the whole ordeal.

It took a few days for me to fully take in what had happened. Fortunately, I was fine to carry on playing after getting two weeks off, but I think it must have affected my form because the next rugby I played was for England in that Autumn series in which I really struggled and was eventually dropped. With hindsight, I probably wasn't ready to play even though I felt fine. Perhaps there were some psychological scars which hadn't healed.

Going through something like that was definitely a reminder of how fragile this whole professional career can be. My dad has it right when he talks about how much the game has changed now in terms of its physicality and the increased dangers that therefore exist for us players.

At least he can actually watch me play though, unlike my mum who prefers to watch on TV as she finds it too stressful to be at the game. My grandma's even worse though – she won't even watch me play on telly, because she can't stand seeing those big hits. Every time there's impact she screams and everyone else watching then screams at her 'Get out!' So she's left in another room shouting out 'What's the score?' and waiting for updates from someone in the TV room.

She can't deal with it at all, but in a weird way I do kind of understand where she's coming from. I think that knowing that the huge injury risks are a stark reality of playing rugby today, even for all its amazing rewards that are now available, is definitely a sobering thought. But that makes it absolutely essential for me to be able to relax and unwind whenever I need to. And I don't mean sitting at home with my pipe and slippers; I haven't become a boring old man overnight. For all my maturity and con-scientiousness as a rugby player these days, I still need to go out and have a good time just like everyone else – just like *you* would do after a tough week at work.

This is not an excuse for me to go as wild as I can as often as possible, but I think relaxing and cutting loose a bit is as important as all the hard work I have to do as a pro and gives me that balance. And, as luck would have it, I really do enjoy going out and having fun.

Occasionally, the old gang will have a get-together back in Wales. I love going out there – before Josh moved to Sydney, me, him, Toby, Mako and Maka would do the odd weekend in Pontypool for old time's sake. I was always the best behaved member of the gang as I rarely drink when I go out. I'd usually be on the Red Bull or something like that just to give me an extra bit of energy. But it was hardly needed as I'm always up for fun. The boys would laugh so hard, because they'd all be drinking and then we'd go to a club. Yet the minute we walked in there, they would look at me going berserk on the dance floor, strutting my stuff, and then wonder to each other how it was that the person who hadn't touched a drop, seemed drunker than everyone else put together.

It's not showing off, but if I'm happy I just like to run with it and have a good time. The other boys are much more cautious and think other people are going to laugh at them for dancing, but that's just not something I would ever care or even think about when I'm out having a good time.

But since Josh moved to Sydney, I always feel like something's missing whenever I go out with the gang as he and I have always been so close. We had some great times together, most memorably one summer when we went up to Beverley for the weekend to see my cousin Sam, who we know by his nickname Poundshop. There's no real reason for this other than his name in Tonga is Bownie and my sister was working at a Poundshop at the time and Bownie sounds a bit like Poundie, so we started calling him Poundshop. Admittedly, not the best nickname in the world but it stuck.

He and Maka were studying up there so we arrived there on a Friday, had a couple of good nights out and were ready to head back on Monday, until the boys persuaded us to stay a few more days. Josh and I are quite impulsive and spontaneous, so maybe that's why we get on well. Deciding to stay in Beverley was a no brainer.

I'd booked a train back but I waived it until Thursday – we were having a good time. I remember taking on this burger eating challenge up there where I had to eat three burgers in a burger bun, with two chicken schnitzels on top of it, wrapped up with bacon, and above the buns were around eight onion rings and a whole plate of chips. If you didn't finish it you paid

£30, otherwise you got it for just a fiver. We fully backed ourselves to do it, went for it and got our rewards. You can get away with that kind of thing during the summer when there's no training.

By the time it came around to Thursday we'd been in Beverley for a week but we weren't ready to leave yet. So we changed our train tickets again, stuck around for another day and wound up randomly going on a stag do of a rugby team-mate of Poundshop's who we didn't even know. A few people were asking 'Who the hell are these two?' but we just got involved. In fact, we got so involved that we ended up going to this guy's wedding the next day! He told Poundshop to bring us along, so on Saturday morning we had to dash around the shops and pick up shirts and trousers for the big day of our new best friend, whom we'd only met twenty-four hours earlier.

We had a blast at the wedding, tore up the dance floor and then had another night out before finally returning home on Sunday – although Josh was talking about moving to Beverley permanently until I told him he was being soft. It is the sort of thing I can't really do anymore – having a ten-day blowout that is, not moving to Beverley – and not just because Josh has left the country. He came back for his wedding though and asked me to be his best man, an honour I took very seriously because it led to the very rare occurrence of me having a drink.

We were up in Edinburgh for his stag do, and it was one of those ridiculous situations where everyone was laying into him, and lining up an absurd number of drinks for him to take care of. Being his best man, I decided I had to help him out. The guy was getting married the following week and it was my duty to at least give him a bit of assistance. He was in a fair bit of trouble as he'd downed around six bottles of rosé wine in little more than an hour, but the boys were not happy as they'd bought him more to drink. So I just picked up the next bottle, necked it in one, and went on to have the best night of my life! I did it strictly for Josh, making the decision that my best man duties extended to breaking the habit (or non-habit) of a lifetime. Josh, who had never seen me drink before, was utterly amazed. It was a fun night, but I'm not sure I'd ever do it again.

The wedding itself was back in Wales but was still a classically Tongan affair, with Josh excelling in his skills of disorganisation. We probably didn't help by going out the night before, so we were running a bit late the following morning when we left the hotel and turned up at Toby's house to pick up our wedding suits that he'd hired for us. I'm not sure if Wales was ready for the suit and flip flops look yet, but we rocked it all the same. The only slight problem for Josh was that his trousers didn't fit him, as he must have put on a few pounds since the fitting. So Toby went to pick him up a new pair, dropped them off to his brother at the house and we all headed to the wedding venue. By this time, things were running very late, just like they would in Tonga. Josh's bride Moanna had arrived in her limo and was forced to circle the area because her groom had yet to show up. Suddenly, my phone rang and it was Josh.

'Mate, where are you? Come and pick me up, I don't have a lift!'

'How did you not organise this?' I said with exasperation as I headed off to the car to go and get him. It turned out that not only was Toby meant to take a new pair of trousers to his brother, but he was also supposed to stick around and give him a lift to his wedding – not leave him to make his own way there.

I picked him up, he got married and it was a great day and night, but I had to head back home as I was due to get a flight to Newcastle for a game the following day. On my way back, my phone rang and it was Josh.

'Bill, have you still got your hotel room?'

'Yeah, why?'

'Oh, I didn't book a hotel.'

Unbelievable.

Epilogue

When I stop and think about it, so much has happened in what seems like such a short space of time, that it's often difficult for me to take it all in. I've done so much, yet I feel like there's still so much for me to do.

I spent so much of my childhood playing rugby against kids who were much older than me, and even now I sometimes feel about four or five years older than I actually am.

I think it's because I've had to learn a hell of a lot over the years that I feel like I have the mental capacity and experience of a more senior pro. Whether it's the setbacks I've been through, the successes I've had, or even all the daft stuff I got up to when I was slightly less mature than I am now, they all made me learn so much. In some ways, that's a pretty cool thing for me, but it can also be a bit of a burden weighing me down.

Whatever it is, the bottom line is that I'm so lucky to be where I am right now. And I say that even after having to take myself out of the 2017

Lions tour to New Zealand because of a shoulder injury, which was one of the hardest calls I've had to make. Sometimes, my body just can't keep up with all the demands I place on it, and that's just the nature of the beast. The injury was something that happened a long time before the tour. I tried to tough it out but the timing wasn't right for me on that occasion.

Because of that, my conscience told me that I shouldn't go on the tour, because otherwise I'd be letting people down. I'm not saying that from a selfish point of view, as if I wanted to go to New Zealand and be the star. But I didn't think I'd be able to help the team in a positive way on the pitch. What was the point in touring if I was just going to be a hindrance?

Having learned from so many experiences, I'm now at a stage where I'm confident in what I stand for and what I believe in, so I have no doubts that I made the right decision. And it was *my* decision. It was important for me to show that I was mature enough to make the call myself and not wait for somebody else to do it for me.

What helped me out massively was the realisation, which I'd had a couple of years before, that I should never define myself by rugby – there really are more important things in life. When I die, I don't want to be remembered for whether I went on a Lions tour or not. I'd much rather be known for whether I was a kind or honest person. To me, that's way more important.

There's an absolute stack of rugby still on the horizon in any case, with a World Cup around the corner and loads more Six Nations and Saracens action to come.

So I can't look at it in any other way than I'm in a privileged position. This doesn't happen to most Tongans. My path to get here has had its fair share of difficulties and I've struggled with culture clashes here and there. Coming from a poorer background has also meant that I've not always been able to do whatever I wanted, but that's also taught me the most valuable lessons.

Honestly, I wouldn't have had it any other way, because it's been the most awesome journey. And I'm nowhere near done yet.

AUTHOR'S ACKNOWLEDGEMENTS

I never imagined I would write a book; it kind of fell on my doorstep and for that I have to thank God – not just for this book, but also for all the opportunities I've had in my life so far.

I owe a huge debt of gratitude to my mum and dad for all the time and effort they've put into helping me, and for loving me enough to be able to discipline me whenever I was wayward as a child, to make sure I stayed on the straight and narrow.

I also want to thank my brother, sisters and cousins, for making life so much fun. Growing up together and always being so close was such a memorable experience that will stay with me forever.

To everyone who took the time to help me throughout my career so far, I also want to say a big thank you. There are so many people I crossed paths with who would share things with me and vice versa – it's only a small portion of all the help I had growing up, but I am so grateful to all those people.

A big thank you to Jonathan Taylor and everyone at Headline for giving me this chance – there are so many other rugby players they could have chosen, but they chose me. I'd also like to acknowledge all the work done by Gershon Portnoi in helping me to write this book; I hope you'll agree with me that he did a great job.

Finally, thanks to my agent Adam Phillips at Wasserman, for making all of this happen. He's always pushing me to do stuff I never want to do, but I'm so glad I chose to do this because it shows people I'm a little bit different to the person they see on the pitch, right? Right!

PICTURE CREDITS

Supplied by the author: p.1; p.2

Press Association Images: p.3 top (Barrington Coombs/PA Archive); p.5 centre (Charlie Forgham-Bailey/Sportimage)

Getty Images: p.3 bottom (Matthew Lewis); p.4 centre (Tom Shaw); p.4 bottom (David Rogers); p.5 top (David Rogers); p.6 centre (David Rogers); p.6 bottom (David Rogers); p.7 centre right (David Rogers/RFU); p.7 centre left (Michael Steele); p.7 bottom (David Rogers); p.8 centre left (David Rogers); p.8 bottom (David Rogers)

Rex by Shutterstock: p.4 top (Kamran Jebreili/AP); p.6 top (Patrick Khachfe/JMP); p.7 top (Julio Pantoja/AP)

Action Images: p.5 bottom (Ed Sykes Livepic)

INPHO: p.8 top (Billy Stickland); p.8 centre right (Billy Stickland)

INDEX

Abu Dhabi 168–73, 189
Acton 32
All Blacks 21, 232
Argentina 143, 151, 192, 215–9
Australia 84–5, 117, 155, 156, 206, 226–8, 230–5

Bath 189
Berry, Nick 170
Beverley 265–6
breakfast, importance of 39
Bristol 28, 55, 112–3, 116–7, 132–3, 203, 241–2
Bristol Colts 64–6
Bristol Schools 56
Bristol Under-17s 137
British Empire 7–8
Bryanston 57

Caerleon 26
carbs 38–9
Carter, Rich 93, 94, 95, 98
Castle School, Bristol 28, 42–64, 92–100, 102–3, 108–12, 114–5, 192
Champions League final, 2008 100–1
Charlton, Bobby 100–1
Chelsea FC 100–1
Chew Valley 64–5
chocolate 28–9

Christmas 29
Clifton College 55–6
Coulson, Jesse 115, 172, 174, 186, 190
Croft, Tom 221, 221–2
Cruden, Aaron 198
Cwmbran 118

Daily Mail Cup 55–6
Dallaglio, Lawrence 189, 241–2
Denver 229
Dickson, Karl 169
Doyin (management company representative) 231–6
Doyle, JP 165–6
Dubai 227–8

East Wales Schools Under-11s 46, 55
Easter, Nick 231, 232, 233, 234
Ebbw Vale 104, 105
Edinburgh 266–7
England national team 116–7, 118, 198–9, 201, 206, 215–22, 223, 224–5, 226–9, 236
England Rugby Football Union 152
England Under-18s 35, 99, 134–5, 137, 144–60, 166, 186–7, 188, 193–7
Eton 58
European Challenge Cup 250
European Cup 198, 201, 226

Facebook 205
Faletau, Josh 60–3, 64, 100, 107, 112–4, 219, 264–5, 266–8
Faletau, Moanna 267
Faletau, Taulupe (Toby) 5, 50, 60–4, 107, 112–4, 155, 204, 219, 220, 248, 264–5, 267
Farrell, Owen 145–6, 150
fat burner sessions 30
Fiji 73
Filton College 113
Fletcher, John 35, 186
food and diet 26–31, 35, 36–41, 178–80, 247, 254, 255
Ford, George 145–6, 154

Gibbons, Charlotte 35, 146, 157, 159–60
Gordon, Jane 118–20
Gordon, Terry 'Tiger' 116, 118–20, 167
Grand Slam, 2016 206, 223, 224–5, 236
Griffiths, Eddie 245, 252, 253
Gwent 55

Harlequins 169–70
Harrow Glees 192
Harrow School 115, 155, 165–6, 172–7, 178, 180, 185–9, 190, 191–2
Haskell, James 221, 247
Hertfordshire University Freshers' Week 229–30, 235
High Wycombe 32, 173, 189, 252

injuries 63, 141–3, 155–7, 200, 256, 270
Italy 90

Jason (friend) 106
Jones, Dawson 'Uncle Daws' 37, 116, 118, 167
Jones, Eddie 225
Jones, Sam 148
Joseph, Jonathan 154

Kingsley-Jones, Phil 19, 20
Kruis, George 40

Lambert, Mark 170–1
Lancaster, Stuart 221
Leeds 189, 220, 221
Leinster 250
Lewsey, Faletau, Josh 241–2
Lomu, Jonah 19, 117–8
London Irish 58–9

Lowe, George 169

McDonald's 23–6, 26, 208
Maka, Anthony 64, 100, 112–4, 121–9, 153–4, 229, 265–6
Mallett, John 58
Manchester United 100–1
Marmaris, Pontypool kebab shop 29–30
Millfield 57–8, 172–3, 188
Munster 256–62

New Panteg Under-11s 4–5
New Zealand 27, 82–3, 195, 198–9, 206, 270
Newcastle Upon Tyne 154
Newport Gwent Dragons 63, 220
Newport High School Old Boys 26, 47
Northampton 198

O'Connell, Paul 263
Ojo, Topsy 58–9
O'Leary, Helen 213, 252

Paris 206
Payne, Alex 231–5
Pennyhill Park 221
Pontypool 5, 7, 8, 19, 21, 29–30, 239–41, 242, 264–5
Pontypool Schools team 116
Pontypridd 15, 21
Premiership 226, 229, 248–9
prop 49–50

Racing 92 201
racism 122–9, 130
referees 160–6
religion 6–7, 27, 55, 73, 177, 191–2, 196–7, 202, 202–4
Rosslyn Park 58–9
Rowntree, Graham 219–20, 222

Sam (cousin) 265–6
Samoa 73, 194, 199
Saracens 37, 40, 177, 195, 198, 201, 208, 226, 229
    BV's move to 248–53
    Mako at 199–200, 248–9, 252
    medical staff 263
    Munster, 2014 256–62
    talks with 244–6
    training and ethos 253–6
school dinners 28, 80

Scotland 118, 154, 230–5
Simmone (girlfriend) 38–9, 229
Sinclair, Malcolm 252
Six Nations, 2013 219
Six Nations, 2016 118, 206
Sky Sports 231–5
sleeping patterns 39
Smart, Mr 97–8
Société Générale 230
Sofia 231–5, 236
South Africa 19, 155–6
South Gloucestershire championship 65
South West Academies 148, 153–4
Spacey, Lloyd 28, 42–6, 48, 56, 57, 58,
     58–9, 110, 111–2, 115, 160,
     162, 167
Spurling, Scott 177, 188
stick rugby 86–90
Stoke Mandeville Hospital 36
Surrey Sevens tournament, 2010 188–9
Sydney 264

Taplin, Ian 179–80, 181–5, 212–3
Taylor, Marcus 114–5
Taylor, Neil 154–5
Thornbury 113, 121–9, 203
Thornbury Park 154–5
Toa Ko Maafu 72
Tonga 19, 21, 54–5, 109, 158, 203, 206,
     250–1
  attitudes 73
  BV's connection with 90–1
  BV's life in 66–84
  comparison with UK 72–3
  islands 71
  kava ceremony 74
  Longo Longo 71–2
  Nuku'alofa 85
  schools 66–71, 75–81, 86–90
  side school 75–80, 85–6
  Sundays 27, 73
  village team 72
Tonga national team 214–5
Tongatapu 71
Toulon 198, 201
training
  BV's childhood 1–6, 12–7, 98, 131–41,
     162–5
  fat burner sessions 30
  Saracens 253–6
  Wasps 177–85
Tuilagi, Brian 229

Tuilagi, Manu 154
Twickenham 189, 214–5, 229

United Arab Emirates 168–73

Vunipola, Ana 8, 115, 206, 207
Vunipola, Billy
  arrival in Britain 22, 238–9
  arrival in Pontypool 239–41, 243
  BB gun incident 92–9, 101
  bike incident 103–7
  brain scare 209–13
  cartilage operation 143
  celebrity 241
  childhood 1–22, 112–4, 121–31, 269
  childhood training 1–6, 12–7, 98,
     131–41, 162–5
  concussion, 2014 256–63
  connection with Tonga 90–1
  contact game 46–8
  cousins 244
  debt to mother 36
  decision to be rugby player 17–8
  discipline 6, 9–11, 12, 96–7, 101–2,
     106–12
  early years in Tonga 66–84, 85–90
  earnings 90–1
  education 9–10, 13, 92–100, 108–12,
     114–6
  England call up 219–22
  England debut 215–9
  family support 204–8
  fathers aspriations for 12
  food and diet 26–31, 35, 36–41,
     178–80, 247, 254, 255
  at Harrow 172–7, 178, 180, 185–9, 190,
     191–2
  impulsive acts 92–113
  Josh's wedding 266–8
  journey 270–1
  knee injury, 2015 228, 229, 232, 233–5
  knee injury, 2016 247
  knee injury, 2017 40
  knee surgery, 2016 207–8
  loss of faith 193–201, 208–9
  maturity 269–70
  motivation 158–9
  move to Saracens 248–53
  Munster, 2014 256–62
  outlook 222–6, 255
  physique 43, 46, 48–9, 53–5, 56, 64
  pneumonia and discitis 30–6

Vunipola, Billy — *cont.*
 pro debut 168–73
 religious background 6–7, 27, 55, 73,
  177, 191–2, 196–7, 202, 202–4
 Saracens training and ethos 253–6
 school rugby 42–64, 160–7, 188–9
 signs for Wasps 246–7
 sleeping patterns 39
 talks with Saracens 244–6
 Tongan lifestyle 6–7, 11
 Under-18 rugby 64–6
 Wasps training sessions 177–85
 weight 26, 27–8, 30–1, 32, 41,
  43, 49, 150–1, 155, 179–80,
  258–9, 262
Vunipola, Fe'ao
 arrival in Britain 19–21, 118–9
 arrival in Pontypool 8
 aspirations for sons 12
 attitude to injuries 142–3
 BB gun incident 95, 97–8, 99, 101
 brothers 109, 139
 BV's move to Saracens 248–53
 CEO of Tonga Rugby 90–1
 Champions League final, 2008 100–1
 coaches Bristol Colts 64
 decision to stay in Britian 22
 discipline 9–10
 and England Under-18s 152–3
 family joins in Pontypool 239–40, 243
 food and diet 37
 and Harrow 173–4
 and injuries 143, 156
 life in Tonga 74–5, 81–2, 83–4
 life plan 18–9
 New Zealand scholarship 82–3
 Parents Evening 108–9
 plan to scare from rugby 17–8
 on respect 101–2
 rugby career 19–21, 21–2, 139–42,
  214–5, 242–3, 250–1
 support for BV 196–7, 206–7
 talks with Saracens 245–6
 training sessions 1–4, 5–6, 13–7,
  131–41, 161–5
 view of Britishg Empire 7–8
Vunipola, Iesinga 1–4, 6, 8–11, 14, 102
 arrival in Britain 238–9
 arrival in Pontypool 8, 243
 BB gun incident 96–7
 BV's debt to 36
 and BV's hospitalization 35–6

 food and diet 37
 job as a minister 55, 203–4
 life in Tonga 74–5, 83–4
 New Zealand scholarship 82–3
 Parents Evening 108–9
 support for BV 196–7, 206–8
 and training 139
 unable to watch 263–4
Vunipola, Mako
 arrival in Britain 8, 238–9
 BV bike incident 107
 and BV's loss of faith 195–7
 childhood 11, 121–9, 243
 childhood training 1–4, 4–5,
  12–7
 early years in Tonga 85–6
 England Under-18s 151–2, 154–5
 food and diet 37
 Grand Slam, 2016 206
 at Millfield 173
 religious background 8–9
 revisits Pontypool 264–5
 at Saracens 199–200, 248–9, 252
 school rugby 46, 50, 51–4, 57, 58,
  59–62, 64
 smarts 100
 visits BV in hospital 35
Vunipola, Sione 21–2, 81, 84–6, 131,
  139–41, 205–6, 242, 243, 244
Vunipola, Tiffany 8, 115, 207

Wade, Christian 154
Wales 8, 21, 202–3, 228
Walton, Peter 35, 146–7, 151, 153, 154–5,
  157–9
Wasps 63, 168–73, 177–85, 189–91, 195,
  198, 210, 213, 219–20, 241–2,
  246–8, 248–51
WhatsApp 90
Wilkinson, Jonny 117, 201
Williams, Ali 230–1, 232, 236–7
Williams, Ross 46
Worcester 137
World Cup 19
World Cup, 1999 28, 112, 214–5
World Cup, 2003 117
World Cup, 2015 228–35
Wray, Jackson 40
wrestling 12–4
Wycombe Hospital 33–6

Yarde, Marland 218